THE WORLD-VIEW OF JESUS

THE
WORLD-VIEW
OF JESUS

by

ELMER W. K. MOULD, Ph.D.

*Professor of Biblical History and Literature
in Elmira College*

HARPER & BROTHERS PUBLISHERS

NEW YORK AND LONDON

To

MY WIFE AND DAUGHTER

Lovely and Pleasant in Their Lives
Helpers of Mine Own Self
and My Joy

ACKNOWLEDGMENTS

THE author hereby gratefully acknowledges permissions granted by the University of Chicago Press to print the quotations from *The Bible, An American Translation* and from E. D. Burton, *Christianity in the Modern World* which are cited in the notes as from those works; by Harper & Brothers to print the quotations from James Moffatt, *The Bible, A New Translation* which are specified in the notes as from that version; by the International Council of Religious Education to print twenty-eight passages from the *American Standard Version* of the Revised Bible; by the Trustees of Lake Forest University to print quotations from D. C. Macintosh, *The Reasonableness of Christianity;* by the Macmillan Company to print the quotations from R. H. Charles, *A Critical History of the Doctrine of a Future Life,* and from C. G. Montefiore, *The Synoptic Gospels,* which are cited in the notes as from those works; and by Charles Scribner's Sons to print the quotations from B. W. Bacon, *The Story of Jesus;* John Baillie, *The Place of Jesus Christ in Modern Christianity;* E. F. Scott, *The Gospel and Its Tributaries,* and Wm. Fairweather, *The Background of the Gospels,* which are cited in the notes as from those works.

FOREWORD

As this book goes forth, the world is in a cataclysm of war and human misery. On every hand is strewn the wreckage of ideas and ideals. What is the truth about life and its meaning?

This situation compels us to turn again to the mind of Christ. He thought his way through to the ultimate reality and the enduring values of life. To probe and appropriate his philosophy of life is to gain the truth that makes us free. To love the Lord God with all one's mind inspired the thinking of Jesus and inspires the studies of all who would have in them the mind that was in him. To share his thoughts is to see life in its eternal aspect and to fear not, knowing that it is the Father's good pleasure to give the kingdom, a kingdom which is righteousness and peace and joy in the Holy Spirit.

CONTENTS

THE WORLD-VIEW OF JESUS

Chapter I

JESUS, TEACHER OF WISDOM

JESUS of Nazareth has forever impressed upon the race a whole series of truths which millions regard as normative for life. This fact rates him as one of the world's pre-eminent thinkers. Should he then properly be called a philosopher? Not in the modern technical sense of the term philosopher, certainly, nor in the ancient sense of the term as the Greeks understood and used it. Philosophy is esteemed as the gift of the Greeks to civilization. There is an important difference between Jesus and Plato or Aristotle. The latter, as typical philosophers, were primarily interested in an intellectual understanding of the universe in which we live and of which we are a part. Jesus shared that interest, certainly, but speculation was not his primary concern. His primary interest was morality and religion, and about these his thinking was not abstract, like Kant's for example, but concrete and practical.

The ancient Greeks, however, were not the only ones who cultivated interest in philosophy. It had its counterpart among the Jewish people and was called by a kindred name, wisdom. In its literal signification philosophy means "love of wisdom." Philosophy is not merely the love of wisdom. It is the best wisdom of the lovers of wisdom.

The Jewish people, in the post-exilic and New Testament times, had their lovers of wisdom. We refer to them variously as wise men, the wise, sages, or teachers of wisdom. They were the educators of the day, men whose special interest lay in knowing and producing the kind of thought which is technically termed wisdom. Such sages were usually men of professional scribal training,[1] but a Jew, such as Jesus, might gain a knowledge of the Hebrew language and the Old Testament Scriptures outside a formal school. A man might be a lawyer and have also an interest in wisdom, or a priest, and devote time to wisdom, or neither lawyer nor priest, for there were men without taste for law or ritual who gave their whole time and attention to wisdom, Ben Sira, for example. The aim of such men was to know life and human experience, to find a way to realize ethical aspirations. These teachers of wisdom were the only philosophers that Judaism produced. They were peculiarly Jewish. That they were not after the manner of the Greek philosophers is nothing to their disparagement, nor does it disallow them to be regarded as philosophers. They were less speculative, less theoretical, and less systematic than the Greek philosophers. Professor Toy states:

Philosophic schools, in the full Greek sense, the Jewish sages did not form—they had no speculative philosophy proper. There were, however, theoretical differences among them, especially in regard to the nature of the divine government of the world, and in regard to the dignity and possible happiness of human life. It is probable that a sort of academic life gradually established itself.[2]

Be it noted that the work of the Jewish sages developed contemporaneously with that of the Greek philosophers. These Jewish men of wisdom were recognized as a distinct class as far back as Jeremiah's time, *ca.* 600 B.C.[3] Greek philosophy began with Thales, *ca.* 600 B.C. The founders of Greek ethics were Socrates (469-399), Plato (427-347), and Aristotle (384-322). Epicurus lived 341-270. The founders of early Stoicism were Zeno (336-264), Cleanthes (331-232), and Chrysippus (280-206). Middle Stoicism was represented by Panaetius (189-109), Posidonius (*ca.* 135-51), and Cicero (106-43). In later Stoicism the great names are Seneca (*ca.* 4 B.C.-65 A.D.), Epictetus (*ca.* 50-130 A.D.), and Marcus Aurelius (121-180). From the seventh to the second centuries B.C. there was growing up an increasing body of Jewish wisdom teaching. Of the Palestinian wisdom writings, Job is variously dated from 500 to 165 B.C. Proverbs, *ca.* 250 B.C., gathered together wisdom teachings of several centuries, the oldest from *ca.* 1000 B.C.[4] Ecclesiastes is dated *ca.* 198 B.C., Sira *ca.* 190-170 B.C., Testaments of the Twelve Patriarchs, 109-106 B.C. Of the extra-Palestinian wisdom writings, the Epistle of Aristeas, which contains wisdom teaching, falls *ca.* 130-70 B.C.; the Wisdom of Solomon, 100-50 B.C.; Fourth Maccabees, 65 B.C.- 38 A.D.; the writings of Philo Judaeus, 15-45 A.D. Jesus of Nazareth was a contemporary of Seneca, and Paul a contemporary of both Seneca and Epictetus.

The work of the Jewish wisdom teacher is thus described by Fairweather:

The Hebrew sage, in his treatment of nature and human life, occupies a different standpoint from that of the Greek philosopher. The wisdom he cultivated was of no recondite, academic type; it found expression in the most public resorts (Cf. Prov. 1:20f). Without being an expert in physical science, he sought to arrive at a philosophy of life through the free contemplation of nature and man, of religion and morals. The "sacred" philosophy of the Hebrews knows nothing of metaphysics, and is essentially religious and practical in its aims. It is not concerned to prove the existence of God, for this is assumed to start with; only a fool can say in his heart, "There is no God" (Ps. 14:2). The Hellenic philosopher seeks to read the riddle of the universe by the investigation of natural phenomena; the Hebrew philosopher already holds in his hand the key of revelation, and with the help of this aims merely at a closer understanding of the ways of God and the duty of man. His theme is

[4]

not the theocracy, but the cosmos; not the history of Israel, but the moral relations of men.[5]

Skeptics were not unknown among the Jewish thinkers.[6] Their skepticism, however, did not call in question the existence of God. The author of the poem in Job 28 raises the question, "Where can wisdom be found, and where is the place of understanding?"[7] His answer is, "Man knows not the way of it."[8] "It is hidden from the eyes of all the living."[9] But he hastens to add: "God understands its way,"[10] and he concludes his discussion by affirming the basic axiom of Jewish thought, "Behold, the fear of the Lord, that is wisdom."[11] Despite all the perplexities with which the mysterious ways of providence beset him, Job kept to the sunnier side of doubt and clung to faith in God and in the end was overawed by the wisdom and might of God as revealed in the mysteries of the universe. Agur[12] finds wearisome the fruitless search for understanding; he cannot name God, but none the less recognizes him as the energy back of the phenomena of nature,[13] and he prays to him.[14] Koheleth is the pessimist among the wisdom writers, but even his thought comes to the same issue: "Fear God and keep his commandments; for God brings every work into judgment."[15] Jewish wisdom therefore "is not a view of the universe distinct from God, much less a view of God distinct from the uni-

[5]

verse; it is a view of the universe with God dwelling in it."[16]

Jesus' thinking likewise posited this same fundamental axiom of Jewish thought. No doubt about the existence of God ever crossed his mind. He never argued about or sought to prove the reality of God. He was too much prophet to feel the need of any such proof. Nor did he attempt a systematic presentation of the idea of God. Jesus assumed the existence of God, not because it was traditional to do so, but because of his own inner experience of God. Jesus spoke first of all to his own generation and his thinking began with a truth which all of his generation acknowledged, viz., the existence of God.

Like every prophet, Jesus was a man of insight and action. Weinel well says:

We have grown accustomed to look upon the history of thought as the history of philosophy, and to look for its chief exponents among the constructors of great systems of thought—men who renounce every form of activity. We are mistaken, however, for decisive action rests upon decisive insight. And this we find in its original power just as frequently among great poets and prophets and men of great force of will as amongst thinkers in the narrower sense of the word.[17]

So it was with Jesus. His world-view grew out of his own attitude. "Not learning but doing is the chief thing,"[18] was a basic principle of Jewish wisdom teaching. That principle set the motive for Jesus. Life was something to be lived rather than something about which to speculate or construct a systematic theory.

It is not necessary here to rehearse the facts in the life and career of Jesus. The significance of one fact, however, deserves to be stressed—he was a plain man, reared by and among plain people, who dedicated his life to the service of plain people out of a profound sense of mutuality with such people. Stripped of supernaturalistic and theological overlay, what we have in Jesus is a plain man who was a thinker. The late President Burton, of the University of Chicago, in his discussion of "Jesus as a Thinker,"[19] states:

The title of thinker must be applied to him in the broad and true sense of the word—a man of thought, of perception, of insight. . . . Jesus constantly drew, in his teaching, not from a mind stored with the thoughts of others, but out from the depths of his own thought. . . . Jesus confined his thought almost exclusively to religious and moral themes. . . . His thinking was intensive rather than discursive, remarkable rather for profound insight into the matters with which he dealt than for the variety of them. . . . The thinking of Jesus was penetrative and germinal rather than systematic. . . . It dealt with central and regulative principles rather than with the construction of a system of thought. . . . Jesus was thoroughly independent in his thinking. . . . He spoke to men from the depth of his own perceptions and convictions. . . . The thinking of Jesus was eminently positive and constructive. . . . Its content and final appeal is to reality. . . . With steadfast aim it penetrates at once to the heart of the matter. . . . He bases his claim to knowledge on his relation to God. . . . He himself must forever remain the clear and shining example of possession of truth by insight.

Goguel remarks that the thinking of Jesus is "peculiarly simple and coherent in character."[20] H. H. Wendt said:

His great originality came from the wealth of his imagination and the penetration of his judgment. His imagination was always providing him with fresh material. Always he goes straight to the essential, and he presses it home in the most arresting language he can find.[21]

Jewish literature has preserved to us the wisdom of some of the teachers of wisdom. That body of literature is termed wisdom literature. Some of this wisdom literature is in the Hagiographa, the latest portion of the Hebrew Old Testament.[22] Some of it arose too late to be given Hebrew canonicity. Did Jesus know and use these wisdom books of his people? The gospel records reflect Jesus' acquaintance with Proverbs,[23] with Sira,[24] and with Ecclesiastes.[25] We may reasonably assume his use of the other books. R. H. Charles specifically discusses the Galilean provenance of the Testaments of the Twelve Patriarchs.[26] Perhaps the most remarkable passage in this writing is in the Testament of Gad:

And now, my children, I exhort you, love each one his brother, and put away hatred from your hearts; love one another in deed, and in word, and in the inclination of the soul. . . . Love one another from the heart; and if a man sin against thee, speak peaceably to him, and in thy soul hold not guile; and if he repent and confess, forgive him. . . . And though he deny it and yet have a sense of shame when reproved, give over reproving him. For he who denies may repent so as not again to wrong thee; yea, he may also honor thee, and be at peace with thee. And if he be shameless and persist in his wrongdoing, even so forgive him from the heart, and leave to God the avenging.[27]

Charles comments upon the teaching of this passage as follows:

It would be hard to exaggerate the importance of this passage. It proves that in Galilee, the home of the Testaments of the XII Patriarchs and of other apocalyptical writings, there was in the second century, B.C., a deep spiritual religious life, which, having assimilated the highest teaching of the Old Testament on forgiveness, developed and consolidated it into a clear, consistent doctrine, that could neither be ignored nor misunderstood by spiritually minded men. This religious development appears to have flourished mainly in Galilee.[28]

The implication of this is that the Testaments of the Twelve Patriarchs circulated as a book of popular de-

votion in Galilee in the lifetime of Jesus, much as
Pilgrim's Progress once did in America. People then,
as now, had not only their Bibles to read (or hear
read), but other religious books as well which nourished
their religious life. Causse holds that the apocalypses
were "the popular books of edification of the time, the
books which people read at Nazareth, at Capernaum,
and at Bethsaida, when Jesus was a child."[29] It was
here in Galilee that Jesus and his disciples derived their
religious culture. We infer therefore that the problems
discussed in the wisdom literature constituted a part of
the thought background of Jesus. So did the apocalyptical literature and the thought problems with which
it deals. The earlier apocalypses, Daniel and I Enoch,
were widely known and used in Palestine in the period
of Jesus' youth. The apocalyptists were contemporary
with and co-operative with the wise. The apocalyptical
literature supports the ethical ideal and urges the moral
imperatives of the wisdom literature. Righteousness
according to the will of God as revealed in Scripture
and in the heart of man is the condition of divine approval and blessing, here and hereafter.

We moderns have a large interest in the silent years
which preceded the public career of Jesus. The ancient
Jewish mind, however, shared no such interest. The
life of Jesus was written up in typically Jewish fashion,
with narratives concerning his birth and infancy, and

then with an account of his mature career. That is all that we have, for example, in the biblical accounts of Moses and of Samuel. It is attractive and easy for pious imagination to fill in the silent years. Yet the writers of the canonical gospels have been most reserved in this regard. Luke alone speaks of the boyhood of Jesus, and tells only one event—a significant one for our present purpose. The narrative of Jesus' visit to the temple in Jerusalem at the age of twelve, with his attention to the learned teachers there,[30] indicates that as a youth his mind was engaged with understanding the problems which the nation's religious teachers discussed. "They were astonished at his understanding and his answers."[31] Luke concludes this narrative by saying that, in addition to other qualities, "Jesus increased in wisdom."[32] This important statement indicates that in the gospel-making period one aspect of the appreciation of Jesus was as a man of wisdom.[33]

In the eighteen years that intervened between this youthful visit of Jesus to Jerusalem and the beginning of his public ministry, we may justly assume that his mind continued active and that his keen interest in religion stimulated him to study of and reflection upon Jewish writings, canonical and other. He had three main ways by which he could enlarge his religious experience, increase his theological knowledge, and develop his idealistic thinking.

The first of these was the weekly services in the synagogue at Nazareth, where Jesus was a regular attendant until he began his public ministry.[34] Here he heard the Scriptures read year after year.[35] The Pentateuch was read in a cycle of sabbath lessons completed once every three years.[36] Selections from the Prophets were read at the services, whether cyclically or not cannot be affirmed. Perhaps Jesus in his youth occasionally read the lessons in synagogue. Children were encouraged to do so, as Abrahams points out:

> When a preacher was present, he read the prophetical lesson, and in the absence of such a one the children read it, perhaps at greater length. For the prophetical reading was by nature a sermon, and as the service concluded with a sermon, the prophetical lesson concluded the service when no preacher was present.[37]

The passages read were translated into the vernacular Aramaic. Certainly Jesus would have had abundant opportunity to memorize some parts and to know others. The synagogue was a place of worship and of teaching. "The teaching given was interpretation of Torah on the lines of Haggadah, i. e., for edification."[38] Such teaching as Jesus heard, year after year, in synagogue, was assimilated into his own thinking and forms, in the view of Herford, the common ground between his teaching and that of the Pharisees. Herford writes:

[12]

After all is it wonderful that a man who had grown up from boyhood under the constant influence of home and synagogue, should instinctively use the religious language which was familiar to him by long association, and use it intentionally because he felt that it was true and expressed what he meant to say, although in other respects he diverged widely from the ways of his fathers and set at nought the Tradition of the Elders?[39]

A second educational advantage which Jesus had in the formative period was, of course, private study of the Jewish Scriptures.[40] Whether there was a copy of the Scriptures in Jesus' own home, we have no means of knowing. I Maccabees 1:56f. refers to the possession and use of private "books of the law" in the homes of certain devout Jews, and this was not long before Jesus' time. There were probably but few such, however, owing to the cost of the writing materials. Copies of the Scriptures in the synagogues were available for reading. Other literature was in circulation, e. g., the books of the third division of the Hebrew canon, which were not read in the synagogue services in Jesus' time, so far as evidence shows. The implication is that Jesus knew Hebrew, and this is generally assumed by scholars.

Jesus' thorough study of the Scriptures is evidenced by the way he handled the Scriptures in his teaching.[41] It is evidenced by the obscure passages which he caught up and set in the forefront of his teaching, for example: "Thou shalt love thy neighbor as thyself."[42] This shows that Jesus not only read but evaluated, and out of his treasure brought forth things new and old,[43] for example, the principle of unlimited forgiveness, "seventy times and seven,"[44] as displacing the law of unlimited revenge, "seventy times and seven."[45] It is evidenced in Jesus' reply to the lawyer who asked him, "What shall I do to inherit eternal life?" and then cited the twofold summary of the law; Jesus said, "Thou hast answered right: this do, and thou shalt live." This reply was an allusion to Lev. 18:5, "Ye shall therefore keep my statutes and mine ordinances; which if a man do, he shall live in them." This passage shows the authority which Jesus saw in the Scriptures. It is evidenced again in Jesus' answer to the Sadducees on the question of the resurrection: "But as touching the dead, that they are raised; have ye not read in the book of Moses, in the place concerning the Bush, how God spake unto him, saying, I am the God of Abraham, and the God of Isaac, and the God of Jacob? He is not the God of the dead, but of the living: ye do greatly err."[46] It is evidenced by what he omitted and by what he criticized, because it did not agree with his inward certainty. He totally disregarded the ritual elements. In the matter of sabbath observance he diverged, affirming the right to say how it was to be used for the good of man.[47] On the subject of divorce,[48] he held that Moses' law was given on account of the hardness of men's hearts and was not in accordance with God's will as elsewhere stated in the Old Testament.[49] Burton's estimate is good:

He speaks, not as one who, being subject to the Old Testament, is bound to accept and repeat its teachings, whatever they may be, but as one who, being competent to pass judgment on it, pronounces it good. . . . His approval is of the ethical principles which pervade and dominate the Old Testament, not of all its detailed statutes.[50]

Above all, his personal study of the Scriptures is evidenced by his central attitude toward the Scriptures: "I came not to destroy but to fulfill."[51] Wendt states:

In so far as he had, on the one hand, expanded and deepened, just from the suggestion and constant guidance of the Holy Scriptures, his own knowledge and inner experience of the character, will, and grace of God, and as he had permanently assimilated from the Scriptures such words as harmonized with the revelation which he had personally experienced, and which afforded a valuable confirmation of that revelation, he had thereby the certainty that the law and the prophets were a true revelation of God, and that their authority was by no means to be simply abrogated.[52]

Wilder has well said:

Jesus' use of the Scriptures is represented less as a decisive court of appeals than as an arsenal from which to fortify his own and his hearers' personal discernment in things spiritual and ethical.[53]

In the third place, Jesus, when growing up at Nazareth, would have had some opportunity to hear wisdom taught by the sages. These sages were the thinkers of Judaism. They were less interested in the legal treatment of the Old Testament than were other scribes, less interested in the ritual at the temple, less interested in the administration of government or the law. They were concerned to understand life, to live it worthily, and to teach others to do so. They made a specialty of teaching the people. In the post-exilic period, when the Jews came to believe that prophecy had ceased, the sages replaced the prophets as the ethical teachers and guides of the people. One of the most eminent wisdom teachers, Ben Sira, thus describes the career of the professional wise man:

> The man who applies himself,
> And studies the Law of the Most High,
> Searches out the wisdom of all the ancients,
> And busies himself with prophecies;
> He observes the discourse of famous men,
> And penetrates the intricacies of figures.
> He searches out the hidden meaning of proverbs,
> And acquaints himself with the obscurities of figures.
> He will serve among great men,
> And appear before rulers.
> He will travel through the lands of strange peoples,

And test what is good and what is evil among men.
He will devote himself to going early
To the Lord his Maker,
And will make his entreaty before the Most High.
He will open his mouth in prayer,
And make entreaty for his sins.
  If the great Lord pleases,
He will be filled with the spirit of understanding,
He will pour out his wise sayings,
And give thanks to the Lord in prayer;
He will direct his counsel and knowledge,
And study his secrets.
He will reveal instruction in his teaching,
And will glory in the Law of the Lord's agreement.
Many will praise his understanding,
And it will never be blotted out.
His memory will not disappear,
And his name will live for endless generations.
Nations will repeat his wisdom,
And the congregation will utter his praise.[54]

These wisdom teachers were to be found in the market place, or at the busy street corners, where the plain people were to be found, and there they appealed to the simple to embrace wisdom and to fools to turn from their folly.[55] The teaching methods of the wise are depicted in the book of Proverbs as the doings of personified Wisdom.

Wisdom cries aloud in the streets,
She lifts up her voice in the squares;

At the head of noisy thoroughfares she calls,
At the openings of the city gates she utters her words:
"How long, you simple ones, will you love simplicity,
And scoffers delight in scoffing,
And fools hate knowledge?
If you but turn and pay heed to my admonition,
Lo! I will open my mind to you,
I will acquaint you with my thoughts."[56]

Does not Wisdom call,
And Reason lift up her voice?
At the head of the highways, on the road,
Between the streets she takes her stand;
By the gates that enter the city,
At the doorways she cries aloud:
"To you, O men, I call,
And my appeal is to the sons of men.
You simple ones, learn sense,
You foolish ones, learn wisdom."[57]

In their homes and lecture halls the wisdom teachers gathered pupils about them and taught them wisdom.

Turn in unto me, ye unlearned,
And lodge in my house of instruction.[58]

Look for him who is wise, and seek him out earnestly,
And let thy foot wear out his threshold.[59]

An interesting light is thrown upon this teacher-pupil relationship in Aboth. "Let thy house be a meeting place for the wise, and bedust thyself with the dust of their feet, and drink with thirst their words."[60] The meaning is that pupils were to invite such wisdom teachers to their homes and to ask in others to hear them teach, and more significant still, to follow such teachers about. "He who walks with wise men will become wise."[61]

In view, therefore, of these educational methods of the Jewish wisdom teachers, a greater significance attaches to the statement, "Jesus increased in wisdom."[62] It was such a teacher of wisdom that Jesus himself became.

Jesus thought and taught Jewish wisdom. The spirit of the wise was in him. To consider Jesus as a teacher has long been a commonplace. What kind of teacher he was has not been so clearly pointed out.[63] Jesus is properly to be integrated with the wisdom teachers of Judaism. This interpretation not only does not modernize Jesus, it emphatically orients him historically. "Jesus was the most eminent teacher of wisdom in the first century. This was his occupation."[64] "We often think of Jesus Christ as a prophet, as a priest, and as a king, but ordinarily we overlook the fact that he also stood as the highest representative of the wise."[65]

In Galilee, Jesus' ministry was primarily that of a prophet and a teacher. The most certain fact that we know about Jesus is that he was a teacher. The Fourth Gospel quite fittingly ascribes to Jesus this self-appraisal: "Ye call me Teacher; and ye say well, for so I am."[65A] His ethical teaching shines through every account of his life. He is represented thus in the oldest sources. Mark, though himself chiefly interested in miracle working, clearly represents that Jesus subordinated this element to his prophetic preaching: "And he saith unto them, Let us go elsewhere into the next towns, that I may preach there also; for to this end came I forth."[66] Further, Mark refers frequently to Jesus' teaching, even though Mark himself gives very little of its content.[67] Mark records that Jesus was saluted as Rabbi by his disciples.[68] Mark refers to the long, tasseled, teacher's robe which Jesus wore, on which the crowding people tried to lay hold.[69] This picture of Jesus as a teacher is not one that Mark would have invented. Mark's dominant interest is Christological. His thesis is that Jesus' divine sonship was evidenced by the mighty works which he did. There was no messianic theory to the effect that the messiah would be a teacher of religion. It was one of the difficult problems of primitive Christian thought to adjust the teacher Jesus to the idea of the messiah, for nothing had led them to expect the messiah in the role of a teacher.

The conception of Jesus as a teacher underlies the second basic source of the synoptic tradition, viz., "Q" and its allies. Streeter states:

Q, as far as one can make out, was a collection of the "Wise Sayings" of Christ, comparable to a book like Proverbs or the Pirke Aboth, with very little attempt at arrangement.[70]

Concerning the *Logia* form of utterances in the synoptic gospels, Bultmann writes:

They might just as correctly be called "wisdom utterances," for they are forms of expression which have their parallels in oriental wisdom literature. Unlike the Greeks, the Orient expressed its world-view and its appreciation of the significance of human life, not in systematic philosophy, but in the form of short proverbs often marked by crisp expression, pictorial vividness, and poetic beauty. Such "wisdom" is well known in the literature of ancient Egypt as well as in the Old Testament (the Wisdom of Solomon, or the Proverbs); it was also current in Judaism and was much used by the rabbis (Jesus, Sirach, and the Sayings of the Fathers or Pirke Aboth). Among the Arabs also this type of proverbial utterance was well developed. Many of the reported sayings of Jesus belong to this type of "wisdom" —for example, the words concerning the laying up of treasure (Matt. 6:19-21), or the words concerning anxious care (Matt. 6:25-34) or the utterance: "No man can serve two masters" (Matt. 6:24). Most of these sayings have direct parallels in the rabbinic literature. It is quite possible that Jesus actually uttered this or that proverb in precisely the form in which the synoptic gospels have reported it. It is also possible that he may have quoted certain proverbial utterances that were current among the people. But we must also reckon with the possibility that the Christian community put into his mouth many impressive statements which really came from the treasure house of Jewish "wisdom."[71]

Bultmann does not seem to apprehend the significance of his own statements. To him these *Logia* utterances furnish very little information as to the characteristic historical significance of Jesus, since no essential difference can be discovered between them and Jewish wisdom. Bultmann dismisses the picture of Jesus as a teacher of wisdom with a mere gesture: "If we leave out of account the first picture (Jesus as wisdom teacher) as being the least probable," etc.[72] On the contrary the *Logia* utterances throw clear light upon the characteristic historical significance of Jesus. Even on Bultmann's third (and preferred) possibility that such statements were attributed to Jesus by the "Christian community," this was done because the early Christian community organically related Jesus to Jewish wisdom, which made the attributing to him of such statements historically appropriate. The early Christian community would not have invented the picture of Jesus as a teacher of wisdom, because such a picture was too difficult to fit in with the Christian community's Christological picture of Jesus.

As for the genuineness of the sayings attributed to Jesus, a considerable group of critics maintains that there can be no certainty at all, for what the gospels

contain represents the thinking of the early Christian
community, especially the gospel writers, which they
have put in the mouth of Jesus. When one weighs the
presentations of the thought of Jesus even in the writings of critics of this type (Bultmann, for example),
one finds it too personal and individualized to be really
group thinking. Moreover, we are in no greater state
of uncertainty that we are with respect to Socrates.
Baillie sets this forth clearly:

Like Jesus, Socrates left no writing behind him, and it is,
as a matter of fact, much more difficult to feel certain about
any words actually spoken by him than it is to feel certain
about the words actually spoken by our Lord; yet his hold
upon the thought and life of succeeding generations was
greater than that of any other man whose name is mentioned in our histories of philosophy. The schools which
drew their inspiration from him—the Cynics, the Cyreniacs,
the Megarians, the Academy, and, later on, the Lyceum and
the Stoa—were more at odds about correct doctrine than
have been the schools of Christian theology, yet they were
all as much at one in their attachment to Socrates as have
been our theological schools in their attachment to Jesus
Christ.[73]

Embedded in the "Q" material, which is the non-
Markan material common to Matthew and Luke, are
certain passages which definitely relate Jesus to Jewish
wisdom teaching and represent him as so classing himself. In the extended discourse on the nature of the

mission of John the Baptist and its contrast with his own,[74] Jesus concludes by saying, "And Wisdom is justified by her children,"[75] meaning thereby to classify himself and John as such children of wisdom.[76] In another setting Jesus is reported as saying, "Therefore also said the Wisdom of God, I will send unto them prophets and apostles."[77] Matthew, doubtless more accurately, has it: "prophets and wise men and scribes."[78] With these Jesus quite clearly integrates himself. Matthew omits the introductory words, which make the Wisdom of God the speaker, and understands Jesus himself as the "I" who speaks and sends forth the prophets. It is quite in keeping with the method of wisdom writers to portray some person as the mouthpiece of Wisdom speaking thus in the first person, for example, the "Preacher" in Ecclesiastes, commonly understood to be Solomon, the patron saint of wisdom literature. Doubtless due to the same interpretative process of making Wisdom speak through the mouth of her teacher is the saying:

Come unto me, all ye that labor and are heavy laden, and I will give you rest. Take my yoke upon you, and learn of me; for I am meek and lowly in heart: and ye shall find rest unto your souls. For my yoke is easy, and my burden is light.[79]

That this is characteristic wisdom teaching is evident from a comparison with Sira.

Listen, my child, and accept my opinion,
And do not refuse my advice.
Put your feet into her fetters,
And your neck into her collar.
Put your shoulder under her and carry her,
And do not weary of her chains;
Come to her with all your heart,
And follow her ways with all your might.
Inquire and search, and she will be made known to you,
And when you have grasped her, do not let her go.
For at last you will find the rest she gives,
And you will find her turning into gladness.
Her fetters will become your strong defense,
And her collars a splendid robe.
She wears gold ornaments,
And her chains are purple thread;
You will put her on like a splendid robe,
And put her on your head like a victor's wreath.[80]

The Matthean saying quoted above is an addition to the hymn of wisdom which praises the Father for hiding the mystery from the wise and understanding and revealing it unto babes.

I thank thee, O Father, Lord of heaven and earth, that thou didst hide these things from the wise and understanding, and didst reveal them unto babes: yea, Father, for so it was well-pleasing in thy sight. All things have been delivered unto me of my Father: and no one knoweth the Son, save the Father; neither does any know the Father, save the Son, and he to whomsoever the Son willeth to reveal him.[81]

[25]

Professor Bacon writes:

No student of lyric wisdom, with its appeals to wayward men, and its claim to a knowledge of God given only to his chosen, can mistake the nature of this hymn. It follows the stereotyped form of such lyrics, in which "Wisdom praises herself." . . . The writer of the Second Source places it in the mouth of Jesus because as supreme leader in the divinely given redemptive mission of Israel the Servant is "Wisdom incarnate."[82]

On the same basis is to be explained:

O Jerusalem, Jerusalem, that killeth the prophets, and stoneth them that are sent unto her! how often would I have gathered thy children together, even as a hen gathereth her chickens under her wings, and ye would not![83]

Here then in the earliest gospel sources Jesus is understood as a man of wisdom. These sources depict Jesus as an itinerant teacher. He preached in the synagogues, for example in Nazareth, Capernaum, and elsewhere. He addressed people in the villages, not only in synagogues, but on the streets. He taught them about the countryside wherever he chanced to meet them, by the lake, in the field, or on the hillside. This method of Jesus is characteristically that of the wisdom teachers.[84]

That his contemporaries appreciated Jesus as a man of wisdom is indicated in another narrative. "He cometh into his own country; and his own disciples follow him. And when the sabbath was come, he began to teach in the synagogue: and many hearing him were astonished, saying, Whence hath this man these things? and What is the wisdom that is given unto this man, and what mean such mighty works wrought by his hands?"[85] Matthew reports the same incident: "Whence hath this man this wisdom?"[86] Luke makes no mention of the mighty works; he only remarks upon "the words of grace which proceeded out of his mouth."[87]

What stimulus evoked in Jesus this type of ministry? "He saw a great multitude, and he had compassion on them, because they were as sheep not having a shepherd; and he began to teach them many things."[88] With regard to this Herford states very significantly:

How far the influence of the Pharisees was felt outside the synagogues it would be hard to say. It does not appear that they made any direct efforts as religious teachers to get hold of outsiders, who never went to synagogue. . . . Consequently there were many who were without any religious teaching, being (for whatever reason) not attendants at any synagogue, yet willing to respond to such teaching if it were offered to them and brought to them. These are the "sheep without a shepherd," and these are they to whom Jesus especially ministered. To do so outside the synagogue was something new. John the Baptist, it is true, did not preach in the synagogues; but he remained in the desert or by the Jordan, and people went to hear him or not as they chose.

Jesus went about amongst the people, in the places where they lived, and no one before him had ever done so. He went to them as one of themselves, with a sympathy such as no teacher had ever shown to them.[89]

It was a social interest that led Jesus to go among the masses as a teacher. Such a social interest may have been stimulated in the first instance by the diversified contacts that were possible for Jesus as a Nazarene in the neighboring communities of Sepphoris, Galilee's largest city which was but an hour's walk from Nazareth, and Japhia, the largest village, but a half-hour south of Nazareth. Such social contacts during his formative years make it possible to understand why Jesus was the acceptable teacher of plain people wherever he found them, men and women in the crowded streets of Capernaum, fishermen on the lake shore, laborers in the fields, or travelers on the highways.

Jesus pursued his ministry in the manner of friendship and intimate personal relationship. The synoptic records give a unique degree of prominence to disciples in Jesus' ministry. He deliberately chose this method rather than any other for his work, for it was a customary method with Jewish teachers.[90] He did not write wisdom. He embodied in certain men the living spirit of his teaching. The doctrinal basis of discipleship in Jesus' world-view will be discussed in a later chapter.[91]

It is important to see this conception of Jesus as an itinerating wisdom teacher in a larger social setting. Such itinerant teaching and preaching was a common phenomenon of the time in the Roman Empire. There is some likelihood that the Jews themselves carried on a propagandist movement in the extra-Palestinian area.[92] Of far greater significance, however, were the traveling philosophic teachers of the Mediterranean area. With genuine earnestness and zeal these men journeyed far and wide with their message, calling the masses of plain people to a higher type of life, in the name of philosophy. Such itinerant teachers were popularly called philosophers. The whole emphasis of philosophy in the first century was ethical; its aim was the formation and guidance of moral character. The missionary philosopher was everywhere a familiar figure, with his long cloak and his staff and scrip, addressing plain people wherever a crowd gathered. The crowd often jeered, but listened none the less, and found some help toward a way of life, for such itinerant preachers were not intellectuals, but plain people themselves.[93] Philosophy thus virtually made itself into a religion.[94] Epictetus had a lofty ideal of the Cynic preacher as an ambassador of God.[95] Wenley writes:

From Seneca, when Stoics aspired more and more to be "physicians of the soul," the Cynic element in their teaching reasserted itself. The neo-Cynics, at once products and evidence of this condition, embodied a special phase of general tendencies which were sweeping over the Roman world as a whole. Thus they form an aspect of a social and spiritual movement rather than a philosophical school of the Hellenic type.[96]

We have no specific records of the presence of any of these philosophic missionaries in Palestine. However, in view of their known practices of wide journeying, it would be strange indeed if Palestine were the only part of the Mediterranean world where they did not go. There is certainly abundant evidence for an extensive Hellenistic culture in Palestine and especially in Galilee. Mahaffy states:

As regards Syria itself, Coele-Syria and northern Palestine, we may safely assert that no outlying country in Alexander's empire was ever so thoroughly Hellenized. We know this by many Macedonian names of towns and the renaming of countries; we know that Greek was spoken commonly all through this region, and when we come to consider the ruins of great cities founded then or refounded under Roman rule, we find them not oriental or foreign but strictly Hellenistic or Roman-Greek.[97]

Whether, therefore, any of this activity of the philosophic missionaries was known to Jesus and in any way served as a stimulus to him we are in no position to affirm. What is of significance is this: the craving of common people for ethico-religious teaching was world-wide in the first century. The response to that stimulus was likewise world-wide, including the philosophic missionary propaganda in the Mediterranean area and the teaching ministry of Jesus and his disciples in Galilee and Judea,[98] followed in time by the Christian missionary movement.

From one point of view Jesus was as much a philosopher as any of these itinerant Cynic-Stoic preachers who were called philosophers. But as we understand and use the term philosopher today, it is better to reserve it for those who have constructed systems of thought and whose sole aim was intellectual. We do not, therefore, call Jesus a philosopher. There is a better title for him, which both indicates his genetic connections and characterizes his public career: Jesus of Nazareth was a man of wisdom.

To say that Jesus was not a philosopher does not carry the implication, however, that he did not have a philosophy. Jesus did not systematize his teaching. As a rule the wisdom teachers were miscellaneous, Ben Sira, for example. Such systematization of Jesus' teachings as the gospels present, in the Sermon on the Mount, for example, is due to the gospel writers rather than to Jesus himself. Although he did not aim at the systematic presentation of a world-view, nevertheless a world-view underlay his thinking. "In the last resort there is no ethics that can ultimately be divorced from its theory of reality."[99] It is, therefore, important to understand Jesus' world-view if we would rightly appreciate his teaching. Our aim is to get at this world-view as best we can as we find it revealed in his teaching and in his manner of life, in order to appreciate the basis on which he did his thinking.

For what do we look as we inquire into the world-view of Jesus? We wish to know how he viewed the origin and nature of the cosmos. We wish to know his view of the nature and value of man. What about providence and purpose in the thought of Jesus? Did he regard the universe as friendly to man? What account did Jesus take of evil in the world? What did he think of the future? What enduring values can we find in Jesus' world-view?

Jesus was a first-century Jew and, therefore, the basis of his thought is to be found in first-century Judaism. The form and much of the substance of his thought was characteristically Jewish. Elements of the standard first-century world-view Jesus took up and made his own. Jesus was not an isolated figure in history, something entirely new and different. He was organically connected with the past and the present of his people, the Jews. His world-view had genetic relations with basic Jewish thought.

A modern world-view must not be read back into the mind of Jesus. The only valid approach to the world-view of Jesus is the historical approach. All philosophers have been conditioned by the *Zeitgeist*. So was Jesus. Subject to that condition, philosophers have apprehended truths of enduring value. So did Jesus, man of wisdom.

Chapter II

THE COSMOS

THE Jews, as well as other peoples of the first century, naïvely conceived of the universe as three-storied in structure, comprising the earth, an underworld, and the heavens above. Their universe was geocentric. Of this earth, practically only the Mediterranean area came into view. Of astronomy's revelation of a vast universe of universes of which our own is but a part, the ancient Hebrews, of course, knew nothing; nobody in Jesus' time did. Our earth, with the sun, planets, and stars surrounding, or rather, above it, constituted their cosmos.[1]

The Jewish wisdom writers, the only philosophers Judaism produced, accepted this current popular cosmology and used it abundantly as basic to their teaching. This is pre-eminently to be seen in the book of Job, regarded as canonical by the Jews of Jesus' day, and therefore among the sources available to Jesus for the shaping of his own world-view.[2]

In the primitive and popular Jewish conception of

the universe, the earth was a flat circular disc,[3] though we do find mention of its ends,[4] and its four corners.[5] The earth and the vault of heaven as well, rested upon foundations, pillars sunk in the deep cosmic sea.[6] These pillars were thought to move when the earth quakes.[7] In a variant conception, the mountains were thought to serve as such foundation piers resting in the deep, the agitations of the deep causing the mountains to quake.[8] Upon what these bases rested was regarded as a mystery.[9] Another and keener observation was that the earth hangs upon nothing.[10] The breadth of the earth was unknown,[11] its ends being the limits of light and darkness.[12] Beyond these limits was the surrounding sea, which was, of course, articulated with the great deep.[13] This ocean had to be shut in with doors and bars,[14] for it was a rebellious thing, delighting to storm the heavens and destroy the earth. In the earth were "fountains of the great deep," sluiceways through the earth's crust connecting with the underlying abyss of waters.[15]

Late Jewish literature was actively concerned with the cosmological problem, not however from the point of view of pure objective knowledge of the world, but in the interest of apocalyptic. A whole treatise on astronomy, I Enoch 72-82, is devoted to this problem and attempts to systematize the many Old Testament utterances regarding physical phenomena. In this late Jewish literature we come upon some interesting additional conceptions about the earth. The earth is divided among Shem, Ham, and Japheth, and Shem's portion is the middle of the earth,[16] and in this the choicest region is Palestine, the "glorious land,"[17] wonderfully fruitful.[18] Jerusalem was the center of the earth; Zion was the center of the navel of the earth.[19] This apparently was a popular mode of thought, for Rabbi Samuel the Less, *ca.* 100 A.D., said:

This world is like the apple of the eye; the white in it is the ocean which surrounds the earth, the black is the environing earth, the pupil is Jerusalem, the image visible therein is the sanctuary.[20]

Analogously, Mount Sinai is the center of the desert.[21] This is a not uncommon mode of thought in the history of religion; the Greeks, for example, regarded Delphi as the center of the earth.[22] Enoch, in his vision of course, visited one mountain so high that it reached to heaven,[23] and seven other mountains;[24] also seven rivers greater than all the rivers of the earth,[25] and seven islands.[26] The earth ends at an impassable river.[27] The foundations of the earth were seen by Enoch in a vision.[28]

The terrestrial disk was thought to rest upon a great abyss of water.[29] This mysterious water depth was thought of as the abode of the "monsters of the deep,"[30] the deep itself being imaged as a dragon, or a serpent, sometimes called "Rahab,"[31] sometimes "Leviathan,"[32] and sometimes the "Serpent."[33] Beneath the terrestrial disk was the underworld, called by the Hebrews Sheol,[34] and by the Greeks Hades, where departed souls dragged out a shadowy existence, all connection with the living being cut off.[35] Sheol, also called Abaddon,[36] was a place of utter darkness.[37] In the older Hebrew literature this abyss was thought of as the great deep of waters whose fountains broke up and caused the Flood.[38] In later Jewish apocalyptical literature the abyss was identified with the kingdom of the dead. There was an abyss of fire into which sinners were cast;[39] a subterranean river of fire;[40] and there was also the conception of a "bright spring of water" for the righteous in the underworld.[41] Finally, this underworld is like a prison with doors and bars.[42]

Above the earth was the arching firmament, heaven,[43] which held above it the upper expanse of waters.[44] The heaven is variously represented as a thin cloth-like stuff which may be stretched out like a curtain,[45] or rolled up like a scroll;[46] again, it is "hard as a molten mirror."[47] In III Baruch 3:7 the builders of the tower of Babel tried to bore into heaven with a gimlet to see whether it was made of clay, brass, or iron. The ends of the earth are at the same time the ends of heaven.[48] The heaven rests upon pillars, pre-

sumably the mountains,[49] which doubtless were considered to function also as the corner piers of God's
throne.[50] God's throne is in the heavens,[51] doubtless
conceived as being immediately above the Jerusalem
temple and magically connected with it.[52] The heaven
has its own laws,[53] which naturally are associated with
the courses of the heavenly bodies.[54] The moon serves
as a measure of time.[55] The stars are older than the
creation;[56] they are regarded as ruling the weather.[57]
The clouds are a mystery.[58] In the heavens are various
storehouses for the snow, hail, and rain.[59] From other
chambers the winds are let loose.[60] Enoch saw the
chambers of the winds and their doors.[61] At each of
the four ends of the earth there are three gates through
which the winds blow in.[62] The winds are weighed
before they leave their doors.[63] The lightning has a
special path.[64] In the firmament there are "windows
of heaven."[65]

Sun, moon, and stars travel in their chariots,[66] which
pass through heavenly portals,[67] and it is evident that
they are thought of as their own charioteers. For the
sun there are six portals in the east and six in the west,[68]
and II Enoch knows the size of these portals, namely
61¼ stadia.[69] From west to east the sun returns beneath
the earth,[70] or via the north behind the wall of
heaven.[71] In another conception the sun is a circum-

ference filled with illuminating and heating fire.[72] Sun and moon are regarded as of equal size.[73] Sunlight is seven times brighter than the moon.[74] The chief function of the stars is the regulation of the times and seasons.[75]

There was not merely one heaven, but many.[76] The number varies, three,[77] five,[78] seven,[79] ten.[80] The conception of the multiple heavens is portrayed in II Enoch and in the Testaments of the Twelve Patriarchs, writings dated at or just before the beginning of the Christian era, and therefore reflecting current Jewish thinking in the time of Jesus. The Testament of Levi, chap. 3, reads:

Hear therefore regarding the seven heavens. The lowest is for this cause gloomier, since it beholds all the unrighteous deeds of men. The second has fire, snow, ice, ready for the day of the ordinance of the Lord, in the righteous judgment of God. In it are all the spirits of the retributions for vengeance on the lawless. In the third are the hosts of the armies which are ordained for the day of judgment, to work vengeance on the spirits of deceit and of Beliar. . . . In the highest of all dwelleth the Great Glory, in the holy of holies. . . . In the heaven next to it (i. e., the sixth) are the angels of the presence of the Lord, who minister and make propitiation to the Lord for all the sins of ignorance of the righteous. . . . And in the heaven below (i. e., the fifth) are the angels who bear the answers to the angels of the presence of the Lord. And in the heaven next to this (i. e., the fourth) are thrones and dominions in which always praises are offered to God.[81]

In II Enoch the conception of the ten heavens is as follows. The first heaven contains "a very great sea, greater than any earthly sea," also "the elders and the rulers of the orders of the stars," and the treasuries of snow, ice, clouds, and dew.[82] In the second heaven the prisoners are suspended, waiting for the eternal judgment.[83] In the third heaven are the garden of Eden, the tree of life, and "an olive tree always distilling oil"; in the northern district of this heaven is the place of the damned,[84] which in other conceptions is always underground. The fourth heaven is the location of the course of the sun and moon, the angels and the wonderful creatures, phoenixes and chalkidri, which attend upon the sun.[85] In the midst of this fourth heaven is "the armed host serving the Lord with cymbals and organs and unceasing voice."[86] In the fifth heaven are the Watchers; it is their fallen brethren who are undergoing torment in the second heaven.[87] The sixth heaven contains "seven bands of angels, very bright and glorious," who plan the revolutions of sun, moon, and stars. "And the angels over all the souls of men who write down all their works and their lives before the face of the Lord. In their midst are seven phoenixes and seven cherubim and seven six-winged creatures."[88]

In the seventh heaven is the Lord sitting on his throne, with ten great orders of angels standing before him.[89] The eighth heaven is Muzaloth, changer of the seasons, of drought and of wet, and of the twelve signs of the zodiac, which are above the seventh heaven. The ninth heaven, Kuchavim, comprises the heavenly homes of the twelve signs of the zodiac. In the tenth heaven, Aravoth, is the Lord's throne, and attendant troops of cherubim and seraphim.

Such was the current popular Jewish cosmology of Jesus' time. This cosmology, in its leading features, was in fact not peculiar to the Jewish people. This was the popular world-view among all peoples down to the middle ages. It remained standard in Jewish thinking throughout the ancient period. Jesus did not expound this cosmology. He accepted and used it. The people to whom Jesus addressed his teaching thought in terms of this cosmology. It was likewise the world-view of the gospel makers who reported Jesus' teaching and by them it was assumed to be Jesus' world-view. In making that assumption there is no historical inappropriateness.

How thoroughly it permeated Jesus' thinking can readily be seen by examining passages in which he refers or alludes to earth, heaven, Hades, and various natural phenomena. God he addresses as the Father who is Lord of heaven and earth.[90] The character of earth's processes is basic to certain of his parables, e. g., that of the various kinds of soil;[91] that of the fruit-bearing earth;[92] that of the houses built upon rock or sand.[93] He contrasts men's ethical dullness with their skill in observing and interpreting "the face of the earth and the heaven."[94] "The queen of the South came from the ends of the earth,"[95] and, as in the customary view, the ends of the earth and the ends of heaven are co-terminous.[96] Equally with the heaven, Jesus regards the earth with reverence, as seen in his teaching on oaths: "Swear not at all; neither by the heaven, for it is the throne of God; nor by the earth, for it is the footstool of his feet."[97] Jesus' prayer is that God's will may be done, "as in heaven, so on earth."[98]

Jesus' most frequent reference to heaven is as the abode of God the Father.[99] God's throne is there.[100] Heaven is likewise the abode of the angels.[101] Angels had an important place in the world-view of some Jews. Jesus apparently accepted the current belief in their existence. In so far as he has anything to say about them it is to regard them as models in doing the will of God. They are a conventional part of his world-view, but he is primarily concerned with God rather than with these intermediaries between God and man. There are references, especially in connection with the catastrophic disturbances of the heavens occurring at the Parousia, to sun, moon, stars, clouds, to "the powers that are in the heavens," and to "great signs from heaven."[102] The permanency of the heavens is assumed and used to illustrate the enduring worth of moral values.[103]

It is a peculiarity of the evangelist Matthew that he constantly represents Jesus as using the expression, "Kingdom of Heaven," rather than "Kingdom of God," as in the other synoptists.[104] It was a common mode of expression to avoid the use of the divine name. The only clear instance where Jesus used the term heaven as a circumlocution for God is in the incident of the dispute over the baptism of John, whether it was from heaven, i. e., from God, or from men.[105]

The gospels represent Jesus as employing the popular view of Hades. He uses it figuratively as expressing the lowest possible debasement in the saying, "And thou Capernaum, shalt thou be exalted unto heaven? thou shalt be brought down unto Hades."[106] In the parable of the rich man and Lazarus,[107] the conception of Hades is the same as that of the later Jewish literature, as noted in the foregoing.[108] Both Lazarus and Dives are in Hades, which has two compartments, one a place of happiness, one a place of wretchedness, separated however by an impassable chasm; that the two compartments are in such proximity is a conception quite similar to II Enoch's third heaven.[109] Lazarus and Dives talk to each other, which may represent a current Jewish conception, although we have no parallel for it, or it may be an imaginative element introduced by

Jesus for the purpose of the parable.[110] The place of bliss in Hades is called Paradise in Luke.[111]

The standard Jewish cosmogony is set forth in Genesis, chap. 1. This conception of the origin of the cosmos was common among the ancient Semites, and the ultimate source of the Genesis narratives was doubtless Babylonian.[112] The Genesis story of creation contains some cosmic theory, but the passage was intended primarily for religion. It was read repeatedly in the synagogues, was accepted by the Jewish mind as literal fact and furnished to Jewish thought a kind of worldview. The Jewish mind asked not how, or what, but who. The origin of the world was explained by saying that God created it. The Jews had only a minor interest in what we would call secondary causes. Such modern categories as those of energy, causation, and process were wholly unknown to them. From the viewpoint of science, things happen because they have to happen. From the religious viewpoint, they happen because some person wants them to happen.

That Jesus accepted this current popular explanation of the origin of the world appears in gospel sayings attributed to Him: "From the *beginning of the creation*, male and female made he them." [113] "The blood of all the prophets which was shed *from the foundation of the world*." [114] "For those days shall be tribulation, such as there hath not been the like *from the beginning of the creation which God created* until now, and never shall be." [115] "Then shall the king say unto them on his right hand, Come ye blessed of my Father, inherit the kingdom prepared for you *from the foundation of the world*." [116]

Jewish teachers and writers of wisdom were accustomed to hold and use this conception of creation: "Yahweh by wisdom founded the earth; by reason he established the heavens." [117] "How many are thy works, O Yahweh; in wisdom hast thou made them all." [118] In Proverbs, chap. 8, this thought is expanded to portray wisdom as present with God when the world was created, either as a creative agent of God or as an onlooker:

Yahweh formed me as the first of his works,
The beginning of his deeds of old;
In the earliest ages was I fashioned,
At the first when the earth began.
When there were no depths was I brought forth,
When there were no fountains brimming with water;
Before the mountains were sunk,
Before the hills was I brought forth;
While as yet he had not made the earth and the fields,
Nor the first clods of the world.
When he established the heavens I was there;
When he traced the vault over the face of the deep;
When he made firm the skies above,
When he fixed the fountains of the deep;

When he set for the sea its bound,
So that the waters should not transgress his commandment,
When he traced the foundations of the earth,
I was beside him as a ward of his;
And daily was I filled with delight,
I sported before him all the time—
Sported over this world of his—
Finding my delight in the sons of men.[119]

A similar view is presented in Job, chap. 28:

> Whence does wisdom come?
> And where is the place of understanding?
> It is hidden from the eyes of all the living,
> And from the fowl of the heavens it is concealed.
> Abaddon and Death say
> "With our ears we have heard the report of it."
> God understands its way
> And he knows its location.
> For he looks to the ends of the earth;
> Beneath the whole heavens he sees.
> When he made a weight for the wind,
> And meted out the waters by measure;
> When he made a law for the rain,
> And a way for the thunderbolt;
> Then did he see it and declare it;
> He established it and investigated it.
> Then he said to man:
> "Behold the fear of the Lord, that is wisdom:
> And to depart from evil is understanding."[120]

In Sira also wisdom is objectified. By this writer

wisdom is viewed as an emanation from the deity,[121] and is conceived as eternal,[122] having existed before the creation of the world, and always enduring,[123] a kind of immanence in all nature,[124] and in all peoples, especially in Israel.[125]

Although the gospels do not represent Jesus as speaking in such language, nevertheless this interpretation of wisdom would be familiar to him, for Job and Proverbs belonged to the Jewish Scriptures and must have been well known to Jesus, and his probable acquaintance with Sira has been indicated previously.[126]

A tendency of scientific thinking is to distinguish sharply the natural and the supernatural and to dismiss the supernatural as an impossible category. Neither Jesus nor his Jewish contemporaries felt such a difficulty. To them the interaction of the supernatural with the natural was thinkable, desirable, and to be expected. A first-century Jew who knew nothing about science and had no idea of any such thing as natural law had no difficulty whatever in conceiving God working any miracle he chose. They believed easily and gladly in the miraculous. They did not inquire into the process or uniformity or cause of natural events. They looked upon the world as the scene of God's immediate action. They thought of no order of nature apart from God's will. True, his will and power were seen in the ordinary facts of human experience, but still more in the unusual, exceptional, striking, wonder-inspiring events. The world to them was full of the mystery of the divine purpose and action. Miracles, therefore, were welcomed, for God did what he willed and nothing was impossible for him. Such was the view of Jesus: "All things are possible with God." [127]

It was, therefore, always with a stirring of soul that the Jew of Jesus' day contemplated the outward order of nature. It was all God's handiwork. Reverent affection for nature was a source of inspiration for the Old Testament poets and prophets and sages. It is woven into the texture of the literature they created. That literature nourished the mind of Jesus. Jesus was not lacking in aesthetic appreciation. Boyd Scott quite truly states:

His aesthetical judgments have been very ill preserved in the partial records his followers made of him, but such as do remain reveal a vision in his mind of a supernal glory in nature, and in all who love and serve. But these are but broken hints of an enduring responsiveness which we savor throughout his spirit towards a charm and splendor that lie eternally at the heart of reality.[128]

Thus in his teachings he makes the truth which he is stating plain by some reference to what one observes in nature. The lilies of the field which grow without anxious care teach man unworried trust in God.[129] The branch of the fig tree becomes tender at the ap-

proach of summer; similarly the nearness of the kingdom is evident to discerning minds.[130] A reed shaken
with the wind is a figure of instability of character.[131]
For illustrations he referred in various ways to the
behavior of birds and animals—to birds in nests,[132] and
in the branches of a tree,[133] which neither sow nor reap
nor store their food in barns;[134] to eagles gathered
about a carcase;[135] to the hen with her brood under
her wings;[136] to doves;[137] to serpents;[138] to foxes in
their holes;[139] to wild dogs and swine trampling valuable jewels;[140] to ravening wolves,[141] in the midst of
sheep.[142] In likening his followers to the "salt of the
earth," [143] and again to "light," [144] he called attention to
natural processes as indicating spiritual realities. Fer-
menting wine bursting a wine skin, and a mended
garment tearing apart around a patch of unshrunken
cloth were symbols of the relation of new to old.[145]
The impartiality of nature is illustrative of God's attitude toward men: "He maketh his sun to rise on the
evil and the good, and sendeth rain on the just and
the unjust."[146] His parables abound in references to the
processes of nature. "The earth beareth fruit of herself," is the basis of his parable of the patient farmer.[147]
The growth of the mustard seed,[148] the action of
leaven,[149] the growth of wheat and tares,[150] are all illustrative of God's kingdom.

He was keenly sensitive to the sublimity which is disclosed in the natural order; his mind ennobled nature's ordinary processes by discerning a divine meaning and beauty in them. Nature was to him the living garment in which the Eternal had robed his mysterious loveliness.[151]

Jesus did not speculate concerning the origin and nature of the cosmos. His ideas about the external world were based upon his own personal observation of natural phenomena, which lay open to any plain person to observe, and upon the current traditional popular world-view. His purpose was not to discuss such ideas, with a view to altering or increasing them. Sir William Bragg, President of the Royal Society of London, and Nobel prize winner in physics, has recently stated the scientist's view of science:

The word science has come to mean a knowledge of nature. . . . Science does not include the uses that we make of this knowledge. . . . The right use of science is a matter of morality and religion; science itself is knowledge only.[152]

On such a basis we appreciate the wisdom of Jesus' attitude toward the cosmos. He took what knowledge of the natural world was available and employed it and the popular terminology as the media of the ethico-religious principles which he enunciated. His view of the cosmos was religious, i. e., he viewed all things in the light of God's love and purpose.[153]

It was characteristic of the wisdom type of thinking

[50]

to emphasize mystery. Nowhere does this appear more clearly than in Job. After traversing the whole problem of human suffering, this thinker can only come to the conclusion that suffering is a mystery, just as the whole universe is an unsolved mystery. Suffering is only one of the many mysteries with which the world is filled. In that sublime poem where the divine voice is represented as speaking out of the whirlwind, the manifold mysteries with which creation is filled are recited.[154] Jesus as a man of wisdom shared this reverential attitude toward outward nature. In the earliest sources embedded in the synoptic gospels the central theme of Jesus' teaching is presented as "the mystery of the kingdom of God."[155] The mysterious working of nature's forces illustrates the present, inward working of God's Spirit, unseen by dull or hostile eyes, a kingdom of God which is already in the midst, silent, omnipotent, overtaking those whose spiritual eyes are closed.[156]

The man of science sees in nature that which he can understand. The philosopher sees not only that, but the mystery as well, and it is the latter which sets him his problem. As one such philosopher has put it:

There is mystery—inescapable mystery—about every ultimate fact. We explain as we can by referring facts to other facts; but every new beginning, every personal consciousness, every individual life, all becoming and all being, the universe as a whole and every individual electron, time and

[51]

space, the here and the now, action and reaction, First Cause and Final End, good and evil—all are full of mystery and will be so to the end of the story of human science and philosophy.[157]

So thinks the modern philosopher. So also thought his ancient predecessor, the man of wisdom. It was with the inward aspect of nature's on-goings that he was concerned, and that is where the thinker is face to face with the mystery of the universe.

Jesus' eschatological ideas will be discussed in later chapters. We may here anticipate that discussion to the extent of noting that Jesus looked forward to a future coming of the kingdom of God upon a *renovated earth*. This conception rounds out Jesus' ideas of the cosmos. His world-view was idealistically based. This earth is God's creation. It is the scene of God's beneficent activity, manifested in the usual and in the miraculous. It is to be the scene of God's future and most glorious activity on man's behalf when he brings in fully his kingdom upon a renewed earth. This idealistic outlook upon the world is most important to our understanding of Jesus. It was to him his Father's world.

Chapter III

MAN

———————————————

———————————————

THE Jewish conception of man's origin and nature appears in the two creation accounts of Genesis, chaps. 1, 2.

And God said, Let us make man in our image, after our likeness: and let them have dominion over the fish of the sea, and over the birds of the heavens, and over the cattle, and over all the earth, and over every creeping thing that creepeth upon the earth. And God created man in his own image; in the image of God created he him; male and female created he them.[1]

And Yahweh God formed man of the dust of the ground, and breathed into his nostrils the breath of life; and man became a living soul.[2]

Man is here regarded as having a twofold nature, physical and spiritual. Man's physical nature is assigned a lowly origin, in that it was formed of the dust of the ground, the very term for man *'adam,* expressing kinship with the soil, *'adamah,* "of the ground." Man is classified with the animals in the order of creation.[3]

[53]

Man has "life," i. e., "a living soul,"[4] as have also the beasts, birds, and reptiles. The divine breath became in man a distinct principle of life, so that the life of man became a portion of the divine life.

Man is further described as having an other-than-physical quality of being. Man was made in the image of God, after his likeness. What does this mean? Certainly the divine likeness is not to be identified with the form of man's body, for God is Spirit. Nor does the divine likeness consist in the fact that man has dominion over the creatures, as has God. The divine likeness is to be found in that which distinguishes man from the animals. Though from the physical standpoint he is classed with the animals, yet from another standpoint he is distinguished from them, for of nothing else is it said that creation was in the image of God or after his likeness.[5] In those qualities of man's being, then, which distinguish him from the animal world below him we discern the image of God. This gives man a place of dignity in the cosmos.

The Genesis creation stories represent that a personal creator and ruler is behind all of the universe with its manifold life, and in this universe the highest product of God's creation is man. He is the object of God's personal attention and care. Everything in the natural world was made for man's sake, that he might be truly happy and attain his highest self-development. Since man had need of human companionship, woman was created like man, yet different. In the statement, "God created man in his own image,"[6] the term man is generic, for "male and female created he them." Woman's nature is both akin to and complemental to that of man.

These creation narratives were read in the Jewish synagogues century after century. This view of man's origin and kinship with God was not a scientifically elaborated system and not intended to be such, for its aim was religious and not speculative. It was the standard view of Judaism and it was Jesus' view. He explicitly cited this doctrine as the ground of his argument on the subject of divorce: "From the beginning of the creation, male and female made he them."[7]

Judaism retained a noble conception of the bodily life of man. Paul, reared as was Jesus in Judaism, expressed this conception most clearly when he called the human body a temple.[8] The Fourth Gospel attributes this expression to Jesus also.[9] From the Jewish point of view the body was the visible aspect of the self. For Jesus the body is more than clothing.[10] For one to be anxious about things to wear is to miss the true nature and purpose of the bodily life.[11] Nothing must thwart the spiritual function of the body. "It is profitable for thee that one of thy members should perish, and not thy whole body be cast into Gehenna."[12] "The lamp of the body is the eye: if therefore thine eye be single, thy whole body shall be full of light. But if thine eye be evil, thy whole body shall be full of darkness."[13] On the basis of this conception of the body Jesus evaluated the marriage relationship: "No longer are they two, but one flesh."[14] The Jewish conception of man's bodily nature was sane, for the body was never regarded as necessarily evil or the source of sin. Jesus did not depart from this view. Therefore asceticism is absent both from his teaching and from his practice.[15] When he speaks of those who are "eunuchs for the kingdom of heaven's sake,"[16] he is not counseling asceticism, but expressing the conception of the body as the instrument of higher consecration. As such, it becomes a possible ultimate duty to surrender life in the body in devotion to a cause. In this way both Paul and the synoptists describe Jesus' attitude toward his own death: "This is my body which is for you."[17]

The Jewish conception of the higher nature of man is described by such terms as "soul," "spirit," "heart." "Soul" and "spirit" are practically equivalent expressions for the spiritual life of man as contrasted with the physical life. That ultimate cause which makes man an animate being; that principle of life which unifies and gives meaning to man's thoughts, desires, and volitions; that which constitutes man a *self* is what is meant by the term "soul." The term has reference to special individuality. When man is regarded from the standpoint of how his capacities and powers are organized within the self and how they function, man is called a soul.

The term "spirit" is used, not to designate a different entity, but to designate this same self regarded from another point of view, viz., the ultimate life power from which the self derives its special character. The word "spirit" is used when man is regarded from the point of view of his responsiveness to, or reaction to, the Spirit which pervades the universe, that which Paul so nicely called "the law of the Spirit of life."[18] The cosmos was considered by the Jews to be filled with spiritual powers or principles, good and bad. The spiritual in man is that which is influenced by such spirits outside.

The other term used by the Jews to characterize the inner nature of man is "heart." We must not be misled by our modern metaphorical use of the word "heart" into the error of supposing that in the Bible the term is limited in its designation to the emotional nature of man. It is used without any precise distinction of the intellectual, emotional, or volitional functions, embracing all three functions within its meaning. The inner nature of man is the ruling element of man's life, the source of his principles of action. The heart determines man's thoughts, feelings, and purposes: "Out of it are the issues of life."[19] Jewish thinking did not departmentalize the consciousness of man. Man's psychological being was unitary. When man thought, he thought in his heart. When man loved, he loved in his heart. When man willed, he purposed in his heart.

The Old Testament conception of man's psychical nature was, of course, primitive and popular, not modern and scientific. Jesus' view of man's higher nature apparently does not differ from that of the Old Testament. The terms used—body, flesh; soul, spirit, heart—overlap in meaning.[20] They denominate, not specific functions, or parts, or elements of man's constitution, but rather points of view from which man's nature is regarded. The point of central importance to be noted is that human nature is conceived as a unity. Jesus' view is not dualistic.

In the thinking of Jesus, man is body-soul. The two are in intimate interaction, and man is one. It is erroneous to speak of man's having a soul. Man *is* a soul. This distinction makes difficult the rendering of the Greek word *psychē* into English. The Revised version translates it in the gospels sometimes by *soul* and sometimes by *life*. Certain passages illustrate this and at the same time reveal Jesus' conception of the soul as the center of man's psycho-physical being. "Be not anxious for your life (*psychē*), what ye shall eat; nor yet for your body what ye shall put on. Is not the life (*psychē*) more than food and the body than raiment?"[21] "What doth it profit a man, to gain the whole world, and forfeit his life (*psychē*)? for what should a man give in exchange for his life (*psychē*)?"[22] "Whosoever shall seek to gain his life (*psychē*) shall lose it: but whosoever shall lose his life (*psychē*) shall preserve it."[23] The *psychē* that is thus gained is a higher personal life that is not dependent upon the circumstances of the earthly life for its well being. The *psychē* is viewed as a life principle more enduring than the body: "Be not afraid of them that kill the body, but are not able to kill the soul (*psychē*); but rather fear him who is able to destroy both soul (*psychē*) and body in Gehenna."[24] The highest function of this *psychē*, this inner nature of man, is expressed in the doctrine which Jesus said stood in the forefront of the religion of Israel: "Thou shalt love the Lord thy God with all thy heart (*kardia*), and with all thy soul (*psychē*), and with all thy mind (*dianoia*)."[25] The different terms here used give variant expression to the thought that man's life in its entirety must function in loving God. It is possible to give up the *psychē* for a great cause; "The Son of man came . . . to give his life (*psychē*) a ransom for many."[26]

The word "spirit" (*pneuma*) is likewise attributed to Jesus as an expression for this inner nature of man: "The spirit indeed is willing, but the flesh is weak."[27]

Again, in one of the noblest of Jesus' maxims, "Blessed are the poor in spirit: for theirs is the kingdom of heaven,"[28] the term denotes the "seat of consciousness and intelligence."[29]

Jesus used the term "heart" in the accepted sense. He employed the term sometimes to designate the thinking function of man. "Out of the heart come forth evil thoughts," etc.[30] "Why reason ye these things in your hearts?"[31] The word sown in the heart may be taken away by the evil one, with resulting disbelief.[32] Apropos of the faith that moves mountains, Jesus said: "Whosoever shall say . . . and shall not doubt in his heart," etc.[33]

Jesus also used the term "heart" to designate the emotional nature of man.[34] This capacity in man's being could be perverted and man could "commit adultery in his heart;"[35] or it could be, and should be, sublimated, as the age-old commandment demanded: "Thou shalt love the Lord thy God with all thy heart."[36] "Where your treasure is, there will your heart be also."[37] Genuine forgiveness is from the heart.[38]

Jesus further used the term "heart" to designate the source of man's purposes. "Whatsoever from without goeth into the man cannot defile him, because it goeth not into his heart."[39] But, "from within, out of the heart of man evil thoughts proceed;" thereupon follows a list of sins which arise from evil purposes.[40] "Settle it therefore in your heart," is an expression for determination.[41] The will to forgive is likewise the expression of the heart's activity.[42]

In other connections Jesus used the term "heart" without regard to any one of the specific functions of knowing, feeling, or willing, but rather as a designation for the entire inner life of man: "The good man out of the good treasure of his heart bringeth forth that which is good; and the evil man out of the evil treasure bringeth forth that which is evil: for out of the abundance of the heart his mouth speaketh."[43] Quoting Isaiah, he said: "This people honoreth me with their lips, but their heart is far from me."[44] "Lowly in heart" is a quality of character, i. e., of the total personal life.[45] So also is an "honest and good heart."[46] "The pure in heart" shall see God.[47]

An interesting use of "heart" as characterizing the inner nature is in the doctrine of the hardened heart. When the question of divorce was put to Jesus, he said: "Moses for your hardness of heart suffered you to put away your wives."[48] That such hardness was not the essential nature of the heart is implied in what Jesus hastened to add: "But from the beginning it hath not been so;" even as it is implied in the psalmist's counsel: "Harden not your heart."[49] When his disciples misapprehended his remark about the leaven of the Pharisees and the leaven of Herod, Jesus said: "Do ye not perceive, neither understand? have ye your heart hardened? Having eyes, see ye not? and having ears, hear ye not? and do ye not remember?"[50] He was appealing to something more fundamental in the heart than hardness. That more basic quality Ezekiel called the "heart of flesh."

And I will give them one heart, and I will put a new spirit within you; and I will take the stony heart out of their flesh, and will give them a heart of flesh; that they may walk in my statutes, and keep mine ordinances, and do them: and they shall be my people, and I will be their God.[51]

In all of these elements of his world-view Jesus is in line with the Jewish teachers of wisdom.[52] These teachers were interested in man as man rather than as Jew. The concept Israel is lacking in the wisdom writings. The wisdom literature is universalistic in its outlook and views all men as on an equality. True, the knowledge of Yahweh and of the law is the beginning of wisdom, but the outlook with these writers is not nationalistic but universal and human. They are interested in man's capacities, his potentialities, and his duties as an individual.

The wise men of Israel are in a sense *humanists*. Their point of view is universal and individual; they do not concern themselves with the religious relations and obligations of the Israelites as such, but only with those which pertain

to him as a man, living under the rule of a perfectly righteous Governor of the world. . . . Wisdom represents a
tendency of mind secluded in some way from the main
currents of Hebrew piety, and containing the germs of a
philosophy of life applicable to mankind everywhere.[53]

These Jewish wisdom teachers were in harmony
with the spirit of the time, for it was an age of indi-
vidualism throughout the world. From Socrates on, it
was considered that the proper study of mankind is
man. The ethics presented in the wisdom literature is
accordingly individualistic and cosmopolitan. The aim
of the wisdom teachers was to orient man aright for
life in relation to his fellow men and his God. Jesus,
as a wisdom teacher, was likewise dominantly interested in the individual. The doctrine of the Fatherhood of God was not new with Jesus.[54] What distinguished Jesus' presentation of the doctrine was the
fact that God's Fatherhood was universalistic. Sonship
consisted not in membership in the Jewish race but in
ethical attitude toward God.

A basic assumption of the wisdom writers is that
man is morally free and morally responsible. In the
light of this principle the wisdom teachers sought to
point out the consequences that ensue upon right and
wrong choices. This principle rests back upon the Old
Testament doctrine. It is clearly and forcibly stated in
Deuteronomy:

[63]

Behold, I set before you this day a blessing and a curse: the blessing if ye shall hearken unto the commandments of Yahweh your God, which I command you this day; and the curse, if ye shall not hearken unto the commandments of Yahweh your God, but turn aside out of the way which I command you this day, to go after other gods, which ye have not known.[55]

See, I have set before thee this day life and good, and death and evil; in that I command thee this day to love Yahweh thy God, to walk in his ways, and to keep his commandments and his statutes and his ordinances, that thou mayest live and multiply, and that Yahweh thy God may bless thee in the land whither thou goest in to possess it. But if thy heart turn away, and thou wilt not hear, but shalt be drawn away, and worship other gods, and serve them; I denounce unto you this day, that ye shall surely perish; ye shall not prolong your days in the land, whither thou passest over the Jordan to go in to possess it. I call heaven and earth to witness against you this day, that I have set before thee life and death, the blessing and the curse: therefore choose life, that thou mayest live, thou and thy seed; to love Yahweh thy God, to obey his voice, and to cleave unto him; for he is thy life, and the length of thy days; that thou mayest dwell in the land which Yahweh sware unto thy fathers, to Abraham, to Isaac, and to Jacob, to give them.[56]

This assertion of human freedom is a basic principle with the wisdom writers. We meet it in Proverbs: "He that diligently seeketh good seeketh favor; but he that

searcheth after evil, it shall come unto him."[57] These
Jewish teachers set wisdom before their "sons," i. e.,
their pupils, and then leave them upon their own choice
to pursue wisdom or folly. Sira proclaims this principle:

God created man from the beginning,
  And placed him in the hand of his *Yetser.*
If thou (so) desirest, thou canst keep the commandment,
  And (it is) wisdom to do his good pleasure.[58]

This principle of man's moral freedom and responsibility is clearly stated in the Psalms of Solomon, *ca.*
50 B.C.:

Our works are subject to our own choice and power
To do right or wrong in the works of our hands; . . .
He that doeth righteousness layeth up life for himself with
    the Lord;
And he that doeth wrongly forfeits his life to destruction.[59]

On the basis of this innate capacity of man, the Jewish
thinkers hold man to be responsible for sin, because
capable of choosing the right. Back of their exhortations to repentance and to right doing is the presupposi-
tion of man's capacity to choose and to do the right.

Know, therefore, my children, that two spirits wait upon
man—the spirit of truth and the spirit of deceit. And in
the midst is the spirit of understanding of the mind, to
which it belongeth to turn whithersoever it will.[60]

In Aboth this doctrine of free choice is combined in

characteristically Jewish fashion with the affirmation of divine foreknowledge: "All is foreseen and free-will is given, and the world is judged by goodness, and all is according to the amount of work."[61]

Man's freedom and responsibility is a basic assumption with Jesus. The parable of the house-builders assumes man's power of choice and his responsibility.[62] Nowhere is this doctrine more clearly set out than in the parable of the ten virgins,[63] and in the parable of the talents.[64] The point of these parables is that God's way of rule is to place men upon their own responsibility. He does not impose his will on men. Since men are free, they must be thoughtful, wise, and watchful. God holds them to strict accountability for the use they make of their freedom. So important is Jesus' emphasis on human choice that Bultmann interprets Jesus' whole teaching as based upon "the crisis of decision—either-or."[65]

Jesus "knew what was in man"[66] psychologically. He called upon common folk to "hear and understand."[67] He held that the things of righteousness and truth were self-accrediting to the inward nature of man. "Why even of yourselves judge ye not what is right?"[68] was said to the multitudes, who were just as capable of correct spiritual discernment as they were capable of understanding nature's processes: "Behold the fig tree, and all the trees: when they now shoot forth, ye see it and

[66]

know of your own selves"[69] what it means. Plain people knew where to expect to find grapes and figs, or thorns and thistles;[70] they knew what they did to "every tree than bringeth not forth good fruit;"[71] they knew that the sun and the rain do not select special fields to shine or rain upon;[72] they knew the meaning of "sky red at night;"[73] they knew what salt and light mean in nature's economy;[74] they knew what sort of wine skins to put new wine in,[75] and the appropriate kind of cloth to use for patching;[76] they knew what happened to money secreted away;[77] they knew that they could not add a cubit to the measure of their lives;[78] that they could not make one hair white or black.[79] Plain people knew "how much a man is of more value than a sheep."[80] By all such appeals to their native intelligence, Jesus sought to stimulate the inner nature of his hearers to the right spiritual response. That they were so constituted that they could thus respond is the essential feature of man's psychological nature with which Jesus was concerned.

A noble ethical idealism inspires and impels the Jewish wisdom teachers; this is everywhere reflected in their writings. They saw the inherent capacities of men, the latent possibilities of character. By their instruction, by the sharing of wisdom, these ancient teachers sought to evoke these latent capacities and to help men to be what they ought to be and what they wish to be.

Jesus had this same ethical idealism, the same view of man's nature, ability, and destiny, the same zeal and determination to promote human goodness. He knew the spiritual possibilities of every soul, and this innate capacity he took with an entirely new seriousness. He knew that the prodigal son had the inner capacity to say, "I will arise and go to my father."[81] A sinful woman could "go . . . sin no more."[82] "That ye may be sons of your Father who is in heaven,"[83] states both what Jesus believed regarding man, and what he had before him as his objective in all his teaching. Jesus had the clear insight to see that the family is by nature the social unit. The unifying conception of Jesus' religious ideal is the idea of the family—fatherhood, sonship, brotherhood. The philosopher Plato conceived his ideal as a republic. Jesus, teacher of wisdom, conceived his ideal as a family embracing all mankind.

Jesus valued personality above material things or institutions. He stated this explicitly in connection with the incident of the healing on the sabbath of the man with the withered hand: "What man shall there be of you, that shall have one sheep, and if this fall into a pit on the sabbath day, will he not lay hold on it and lift it out? How much then is a man of more value than a sheep!"[84] No institution, not even the sabbath, equals in worth the human persons for whom it exists. "The sabbath was made for man and not man for the sabbath."[85] In another setting he declared to his disciples: "Ye are of more value than many sparrows."[86] Again, "Of how much more value are ye than the birds!"[87] In view of his principle of the supreme worth of persons, Jesus devoted his entire ministry to the redemption of persons. By his works of healing he redeemed them from physical handicaps. By his teaching of wisdom he redeemed them from ignorance and error. By his friendship he redeemed them from their loss of hope because neglected. By summoning them to a new life he redeemed them from sin.

This devotion of Jesus was not to humanity in the abstract. It was about individuals that he cared, for the reason that he believed they mattered most to God. He sternly rebuked any attitude of contempt toward another person. "Whosoever shall say to his brother, Raca, shall be in danger of the council; and whosoever shall say, Thou fool, shall be in danger of the hell of fire."[88] He was rated a friend of publicans and sinners, and by that very attitude "Wisdom is justified."[89] Individual sinners, such as Levi, Zacchaeus, or a prostitute, received his sympathetic attention because no depth of moral degradation canceled the latent possibility of such a person becoming a child of God. Jesus was concerned about the needs of individuals, whether bodily or spiritual needs. He had compassion on the multitudes, not only to feed them when they were hungry,[90] but to teach them because "they were as sheep not having a shepherd."[91] The worth of persons made Jesus sensitive to the presence in society of those who were wronged by their fellows, the victims of a hold-up on the Jericho road,[92] the victims of a tax collector's extortion,[93] a woman victimized by an unjust judge,[94] widows victimized by exploiters who devour their very homes,[95] the destitute at the doorsteps of the rich,[96] the needy unheeded.[97] The centrality of this valuation of persons in Jesus' thinking is evident from the commandment which he said expressed the essence of religion: "Thou shalt love thy neighbor as thyself."[98]

The seriousness with which Jesus took this principle of the value of human personality is seen also in his attitude toward women. We have at several points observed the likeness of Jesus' views to those held by the wisdom writers. Here, however, we come upon a striking difference. The wisdom writers did not hold or teach a noble opinion of woman. In the prologue of Job, the severest of the temptations to which that sufferer is subjected is that his wife fails him at the most crucial time in his life.[99] The author's view of womankind is: "Man, that is born of a woman, is of few days and full of trouble."[100] "What is man, that he should be clean? And he that is born of a woman, that

he should be righteous?"[101] "How can he be clean that
is born of a woman?"[102] Proverbs considers a good
woman to be the crown of her husband,[103] and cata-
logues many qualities which make up such a wife.[104]
She is good because useful to man. Koheleth's attitude
is: "I find more bitter than death the woman whose
heart is snares and nets and whose hands are bands:
whoso pleaseth God shall escape from her; . . . One
man among a thousand have I found; but a woman
among all those have I not found."[105] Barton suggests
that this was because his life had been saddened by a
woman.[106] Sira is very uncomplimentary to women as
a class.[107] "A woman will receive any man."[108] "He
that getteth a wife entereth upon a possession."[109] The
best he can say for woman is that "the grace of a wife
will delight her husband; and her knowledge will
fatten his bones."[110] His real estimate is: "From a
woman was the beginning of sin and because of her
we all die."[111] Back of this dogma is, of course, the Old
Testament doctrine of the temptation of Eve in the
Garden of Eden.[112] Another suggestion in Genesis,[113]
much elaborated by later Jewish writers,[114] accounted
for the origin of sin by the myth of the union of fallen
angels, the Watchers, with women. One wisdom writer
depicts the women as making the first depraved ad-
vances to these angels,[115] and upon this as a basis he ex-
pands his view: "Evil are women, my children."[116] In

all this range of literature we do not anywhere come upon any suggestion that a woman can obtain wisdom.

There is none of this in the teachings of Jesus. There is no trace of the doctrine of the Watchers, and no faintest suggestion that woman plays a vile role in human life. On the contrary, woman is of worth because she is a person. Montefiore applauds Jesus for championing womanhood. He discusses at much length the question of Jesus' teaching on divorce,[117] acknowledges the defects of Jewish divorce, does not agree with "the extreme attitude, possibly taken up by Jesus, that under no circumstances is divorce permissible,"[118] but adds: "The implied attack upon the inferiority of women in Oriental society, and upon the unjust power of divorce given to men, was of the highest importance and value. Thus, upon the whole, we have to recognize that his words have been of service towards a higher conception of womanhood."[119] Commenting upon the women friends of Jesus who followed and waited upon him in Galilee, Montefiore says: "There can be little doubt that in Jesus' attitude towards women we have a highly original and significant feature of his life and teaching."[120]

Luke, in the incident of Martha and Mary, preserves a picture of Jesus and a pupil who was a woman. Mary "also sat at the Lord's feet, and was accustomed to listen to his word," i. e., his teaching.[121] This is expressed in typical wisdom style. In Aboth we read: "Let thy house be a house of meeting for the wise, and bedust thyself with the dust of their feet,"[122] which means, says Herford, "the disciple should sit at the feet of his teacher."[123]

Jesus' regard for the worth of human personality is further seen in his attitude toward children. Montefiore well says: "the beauty, the significance, the ethical force and the originality" of the gospel story of Jesus and the little children, and especially the saying, "Whosoever shall not receive the kingdom of God as a little child, he shall in no wise enter therein,"[124] can "only with injustice be overlooked, cheapened, or denied."[125]

Jesus conceived of God's object as the bringing to pass of a society of redeemed and God-like souls. Apparently he could think of nothing beyond that. It is in the light of that ideal of a society of "sons of God" that Jesus saw and evaluated persons in the present. The philosophical import of this is well stated by a modern philosopher:

It was in the teaching of Jesus that the worth of the individual soul was first emphatically declared. He carried further the "inwardizing" of the moral values which had been suggested by some prophets, psalmists, and the dramatist Job. For Jesus the issues of life and death were from the heart and the imagination, from the motives and intentions of the will.[126]

The highest point in Jesus' estimate of the value of human personality is his belief in human immortality. That Jesus "brought life and immortality to light through the gospel,"[127] is an altogether correct interpretation.

In the synoptic gospels *psychē* is used eleven times, in what amount to four different settings, in a sense which denotes the continuance of life after death.[128] "Fear not them that kill the body, but are not able to kill the soul (*psychē*),"[129] clearly implies that what ends the bodily existence by no means terminates man's life. "Whosoever shall seek to gain his life (*psychē*) shall lose it; but whosoever shall lose (his life) shall save it alive."[130]

His view of immortality, however, was grounded, not on the essential immortality of the soul as such, but on the moral character of God as love. The thought of Jesus on the subject is preserved for us, significantly, not in a passage of general eschatological teaching, but in a passage presenting his ideal of eternal life.[131] The conventional view of life in the kingdom of God posited a continuance of present conditions and modes of living.[132] The Sadducees assumed that Jesus held such a conception of it. They cited the levirate law to prove that Moses and the law did not teach any doctrine of resurrection, for in making provision to prevent the extinction of a family the law clearly contemplated no such thing as a resurrection.[133] They cited a concrete case to make the doctrine of the resurrection appear ridiculous by showing the confusion of marriage relationships that would prevail in the resurrection life.

In his reply to the Sadducees Jesus taught that eternal life would be free from the relations and limitations of the present life. He based his view upon a spiritualized conception of the resurrection. Such a conception was already in vogue. I Enoch states that the risen righteous "have great joy as the angels of heaven,"[134] and are "companions of the hosts of heaven."[135] Accordingly Jesus did not discuss the nature of the resurrection body or any of the realistic aspects of the future life. To liken the risen dead to angels was to employ the best available term for spiritual existence. What Jesus thought in detail it is impossible to know. He does not speculate about details. He means to affirm full, conscious, rational existence after death.

In citing Exodus 3:6, "I am the God of Abraham and the God of Isaac and the God of Jacob," Jesus presented an argument for life after death rather than strictly for resurrection. He established the principle of his faith in the future life when he said: "He is not the God of the dead but of the living, for all live unto him."[136] If men belong to God they share the life of God. God cannot be thought of as loving and caring for the righteous during their lifetime and then allowing them to be annihilated.[137] Rawlinson well says that these words of Jesus "do give expression to what is probably the strongest of all purely rational arguments for the life of the world to come, viz., that based on the reality of the religious life and the goodness of God."[138]

As Jesus' view of the world of external nature is grounded in idealism, so his view of man's inner nature is grounded in idealism. He sees the ideal as the real, and this is one of the most important elements in his world-view. To Jesus the real man is the man revealed in his capacity for living a moral life in fellowship with God, i. e., the ideal man, the son of God. The sons of God are sons of the resurrection.

Chapter IV

PROVIDENCE AND PURPOSE

THE Jews understood and interpreted the entire course of their racial and national history in the light of the promises of God. The promises were made to Abraham:

Now Yahweh said unto Abram, Get thee out of thy country, and from thy kindred, and from thy father's house, unto the land that I will show thee: and I will make of thee a great nation, and I will bless thee, and make thy name great; and be thou a blessing: and I will bless them that bless thee, and him that curseth thee will I curse; and in thee shall all the families of the earth be blessed.[1]

Similar promises of ultimate greatness and blessing to all mankind were made to Isaac and Jacob.[2]

Out of his love and his beneficent purpose God made these promises voluntarily to Israel. The Jews believed ardently that they were God's chosen people. His promises were his assurances to them that they were the objects of his love and his care, and the agents of his mission. They were sons of Abraham and therefore the heirs of the promises.

This conception of Jewish superiority and privilege developed in two ways, bad and good. The bad effect of it was to build up a national conceit. Some looked down upon other peoples and anticipated the time when they, the Jews, would lord it over all other peoples. The Jews experienced much that might have led them to doubt the promises, but they never did. They were confident that God would make of them a great nation and exalt their name. The more they were oppressed by other nations, the more firmly did they believe that the promises held good and that in God's own time conditions would be reversed, for had not God promised, "Him that curseth thee will I curse?"[3] This Jewish nationalism was ardent and inflammable in Palestine all during Jesus' lifetime. It played about two ideals, passive apocalypticism and aggressive zealotism. The former counted on God taking the initiative in violently destroying their Roman oppressors; all the Jews could do was to await God's good pleasure in the fulfilling of his promises. The latter ideal called upon the Jews to force the issue. This ideal crystallized in the Zealots, the party of revolution which all through Jesus' lifetime and afterward was gathering that momentum which finally broke in the Jewish War, 66-70 A.D.[4]

Some Jews, however, were mindful of the other half of God's promise, "Be thou a blessing . . . In thee shall all the families of the earth be blessed."[5] God chose Abraham that he might through Israel reach the world. Their belief in God's choice of them for the supreme mission to the world inspired them to extend their spiritual faith and life to all people. How did Jews of this type react to the national calamities which often befell their people and caused them to ask, "Is his lovingkindness clean gone forever? Doth his promise fail for evermore?"[6] Such experience, especially the greatest calamity of all, the exile, deepened their thinking concerning God's promises and resulted in the doctrine of the Suffering Servant, of Isaiah, chap. 53. Israel's suffering was explained as penal not only, but more profoundly as vicarious and redemptive. It was vicarious, for Israel suffered on behalf of all the world's population. This interpretation rested upon the old Hebrew conception of social solidarity universalized. It was redemptive, for it focussed the attention of the rest of the world upon the true God. The oppressed and afflicted Servant was bruised and put to grief; nevertheless in his hand "the pleasure of Yahweh shall prosper."[7] God's good pleasure was his purpose as expressed in the promises. The more the promises seemed to be belied by suffering, the more confidently did they affirm their assurance respecting the promises, and project into the future the complete realization of them. The prophetic utterance held good: "I know the

[79]

thoughts that I think toward you, saith Yahweh, thoughts of peace and not of evil, to give you a future and a hope."[8] Such prophetic utterances were made in the face of the fact that all experience pointed to the contrary. The facts of their history were not such as to justify that kind of faith. Its sole justification lay in that confidence in the moral order of the universe which is implied in the doctrine of the promises.

There is no literature which is so saturated with the spirit of anticipation as the Hebrew, no nation which has cherished so ardent and irrepressible belief in its destiny, a people who were looking forwards from a great past of wonders to a future of good and glory.[9]

The doctrine of the promises was part of the Jewish philosophy of history. Bound up in the primitive promise to Abraham was the entire future of Israel. The history of the nation both revealed the content of the promise and its fulfillment in part. The core of the doctrine of the promise is that of an unrealized good which comes to be realized through faith in God.[10] The complete realization of this good lay in the future. Jewish thinking was idealistic. It was the kingdom of God and of his people to which they looked forward. The more intensely their idealism glowed, the nearer did the future consummation seem. The consummation of the divine purpose in history was to be the kingdom of God.

Jewish belief in the promises led them to regard God as the most potent factor in their history. I Enoch, chaps. 89, 90, surveys Jewish history from the exodus on, portraying God as Israel's Good Shepherd who has always guided his flock and will bring them to the pleasant pastures of the messianic era.

Jesus made this Jewish idealism basic in his own world-view. "Fear not, little flock, for it is your Father's good pleasure to give you the kingdom,"[11] well expresses his view. God's good pleasure meant his purpose, all that was contained in the promises. The kingdom, in this view of Jesus, was something to be given. This fulfillment of the promises was not to be earned as a reward, nor was it to be grasped by violence.[12] God took the initiative in making the promises. His was to be the initiative in their fulfillment.

An attitude is a tendency to act toward an object. God's attitude toward man is that of fatherly love which bestows blessings freely. This attitude led him to make the promises. Man's attitude to God is his response to God's attitude. Man's attitude toward the promises is that of receptivity. This is what Jesus meant by the parable of the soils,[13] as interpreted by the synoptists in the explanation they added to the parable.[14] There are varying degrees of receptivity in the several kinds of soil. The same teaching is in: "Whosoever shall not receive the kingdom of God as a little child, he shall in no wise enter therein."[15] The attitude of the child is that of total dependence, humble expectancy, receptivity.

Jesus regarded the present as a time of fulfillment of the promises. "Many prophets and righteous men desired to see the things which ye see, and saw them not; and to hear the things which ye hear, and heard them not."[16] His reply to the delegates from John the Baptist directed attention to facts open to their observation which constituted a fulfillment of prophetic promises.[17]

This philosophy of Jesus determined his attitude toward the eschatological coming of the kingdom of God. He nowhere speculates as to the time of its coming. He explicitly disclaims any possibility of knowledge on that point.[18] Perhaps, as many scholars contend, Jesus considered the time to be short. At any rate his attitude toward God forbade him to attempt to force God's hand. Men might indeed pray God to shorten the time.[19] Montefiore interprets correctly when he writes: "The kingdom would come as a gift. It would be given as a gift to those who were by nature and grace fitted to receive it. The childlike in heart alone could enter the kingdom."[20] In another of his books Montefiore has amplified this point.

The kingdom . . . is not so much a reward as a grace. Do what he will, man never deserves it; do his duty as he may, man has no claim for special recognition and reward. The kingdom, when it comes, will be far greater and more glorious than any man can have merited. It is not the product of calculating justice and retribution; it is the outflow of God's free and exuberant love. I do not think that these few statements go beyond what Jesus actually says in the synoptic gospels, and I am also inclined to think that, though they are not without their parallels in the rabbinic literature, they nevertheless may be regarded as comparatively new and original.[21]

Professor E. F. Scott has stated the matter acceptably:

It is necessary to bear in mind the two ideas which are everywhere combined in his conception of the kingdom. (1) He assumed, on the one hand, as Hebrew thought had always done, that the new order must be brought in by God himself. . . . Man could no more create it than he could make the sun to rise or the harvest to ripen. Its whole meaning was that the world's deliverance would depend no longer on poor human endeavor. God himself would intervene with his all-prevailing power. (2) On the other hand, the coming of the kingdom was impossible without human coöperation. God would not exert his power until men were ready. They were not condemned wholly to a passive waiting. By prayer and repentance and ardent longing they might move the will of God and so hasten the deliverance. They might so prepare themselves that even now they should inwardly belong to the kingdom. In the mind of Jesus these two conceptions merged in one another the more naturally since he thought of the kingdom as above all a moral order.[22]

In the popular Jewish thinking of Jesus' day, God's providential care for mankind was effected in part through the ministry of angels. In pre-exilic Judaism angels as messengers of Yahweh seem to have been identified with Yahweh himself, so that the angel's presence is virtually Yahweh's presence.[23] In post-exilic Judaism, doubtless as a result of Babylonian or Persian influence, angels held a prominent place, as evidenced by the apocryphal and apocalyptical literature. Here everything that transpires is effected through the agency of angels. There are a thousand times a thousand, and ten thousand times ten thousand of them,[24] which amounts to saying that they are innumerable.[25] They are divided into ranks, under the command of archangels. Among such archangels, Michael, Raphael, Gabriel, and Phanuel are the angels of the Presence; they represent God's majestic glory.[26] Angels preside over the nations. At first the angels were considered to be supernatural men; e. g., Enoch became an angel after he was translated.[27] Gradually they came to be thought of as having a different constitution. They are like fire,[28] having a splendor like stars.[29] Sometimes the forces of nature were regarded as angels;[30] hence the entire course of nature was carried on through their agency.[31] Whatever needed to be done in the universe, there was an angel to do it.

The gospels represent Jesus as holding this conventional view of angels. Nowhere does he speculate concerning the names, nature, or activities of the angels. He simply employs this mode of thought to make his teaching understandable to his hearers. In such teaching, angels are referred to as the agencies through which God's blessings to men are ministered. They are guardians of little children.[32] They mediate the mighty power of God.[33] They bear the poor beggar Lazarus to Abraham's bosom.[34] They are models in doing the will of God,[35] and therefore they rejoice over the repentant sinner.[36] Such passages present a consistent view of the angels as mediating God's providential care and blessing to man. Their presence means God's presence.

God's providential care for mankind was, in another view, mediated through Wisdom and the divine Word, which manifest the transcendent God and bring him into closer relation with the world than the doctrine of angels does. His Word is creative.[37] It is sent forth to accomplish his purpose;[38] e. g., on a healing mission.[39] In a "Hymn of Wisdom in Praise of Herself," Sira portrays Wisdom as resident among the Jewish people, which is a way of expressing the doctrine of the immanence of God.

> I issued from the mouth of the Most High,
> And covered the earth like a mist.
> I lived on the heights,
> And my throne was on the pillar of cloud.

I alone compassed the circuit of heaven,
And I walked in the depth of the abyss.
I owned the waves of the sea and the whole earth
And every people and nation.
Among all these I sought a resting-place;
In whose possession should I lodge?
Then the Creator of all gave me his command;
And he who created me made my tent rest,
And said, "Pitch your tent in Jacob,
And find your inheritance in Israel."
He created me from the beginning, before the world,
And I shall never cease.
I ministered before him in the holy tent,
And so I was established in Zion.
He made me rest likewise in the beloved city,
And I had authority over Jerusalem.
I took root in the glorified people,
In the portion of the Lord, and of his inheritance.[40]

Personified Wisdom, as has been pointed out,[41] is portrayed as active among men, summoning them to a life of righteousness. The Wisdom of Solomon traces the working of Wisdom in history as divine Providence.[42] An elaborate philosophy of history is presented which portrays Wisdom as the omnipresent spirit of God in Israel's history.[43]

Thus we observe that God's providence is regarded as mediated both through angels and through Wisdom. The belief in angels has in view the transcendence of God, the belief in Wisdom his immanence.[44] Because it is characteristic of Jesus to look on the inwardness of ideas, he emphasizes the inwardness of the idea of God, i. e., the immanence of God.

This view of God's providence operative through indwelling Wisdom was fully appreciated by Jesus.[45] It is expressed in the Beatitudes.[46] The beatitude form was a well known feature of wisdom teaching.[47] In the beatitude form Wisdom makes her promises to the soul that desires her. Such promises are made without reference to messianic considerations and are promises of spiritual grace to the spiritually minded.[48] There is much in the teaching of Jesus which evidences how basic this religious idealism is in his world-view. "The Father which seeth in secret shall recompense thee."[49] "Whosoever shall lose his life shall find it."[50] "Your reward shall be great, and ye shall be sons of the Most High."[51]

For Jesus, God's promises held good, and his major interest was in the immediate purpose with which God was concerned. In Jesus' world-view God's next great purpose is salvation. Therein he differed from John the Baptist. In John's thought, God's next great purpose is judgment.[52] Jesus in his teaching repeatedly calls attention to factors which evidence God at work carrying out his purpose to save. Jesus adjusted his own life work in accordance with that purpose, and Christianity has

[87]

always understood and appreciated Jesus' ministry as a saving ministry.

Jesus expressed himself in the thought-patterns of the wise not only, but adopted their methods. It is characteristic of the wisdom teachers that they sought out the individual and instructed him, especially the one who lacked understanding. Sometimes these teachers directed their instruction to one individual only. Such a one was called "my son."[53] Jesus worked with and for the individual. It is significant that Jesus nowhere calls a disciple "my son," although in Mark he does in one instance address his disciples as "children."[54] However, he does regard his disciples as sons—they are God's sons. The objective of his teaching is that they may be sons of the Father who is in heaven.[55] Jesus was concerned with God's care, not of the nation, but of the individual. As a son, not of the teacher but of the Heavenly Father, each individual was the object of God's love and care. This was the great assurance which Jesus gave to his disciples respecting God's providence and purpose.

Few passages in the Sermon on the Mount surpass the section on anxiety versus trust.[56] God knows and cares about every detail of man's life and personal need. The world is so constituted that it is responsive to the needs of the birds of the heavens. They have their food and shelter. And man is of much more value than they.

"Your heavenly Father knoweth that ye have need of all these things."[57] "Seek ye first his kingdom and his righteousness; and all these things shall be added unto you. Be not therefore anxious."[58] Bultmann cites such passages as showing Jesus' emphasis on providence, and remarks: "Such sayings in form are apothegms, and as such belong in oriental wisdom."[59]

Among the most significant and best liked parables of Jesus are those of Luke, chap. 15, the parables of the lost sheep, lost coin, and lost son. They all illustrate the same truth, viz., that God is interested in and cares for the individual. This divine grace, manifested in the care of individuals, demands as its human correlative the attitude of faith.[60]

Consideration of the subject of providence and purpose raises the problem: Is the universe friendly to man? This is the way Frederick W. H. Myers put the question. It is not the sort of expression that Jesus or any of his contemporaries would have used. But he faced the problem no less than we.

There are few or none of the major questions attempted by the reflective thinking of mankind that may not be, directly or indirectly, concerned in the answer given to this question. Nor is this true of theoretical philosophy alone; for the principles of conduct and the issues of life, in logic and in fact, largely depend upon whether one says Yes or No to this same question.[61]

In Jesus' time it was common to think of the world as acted upon by Satan and his evil hosts. They were hostile to the higher nature and welfare of men. They filled the world with sin and evil. The earth was the scene of a terrific conflict between the supernatural powers, contending for the control of mankind. Religion viewed God as more powerful than Satan, and had faith that he would ultimately vanquish all the hosts of evil.[62]

Jesus viewed the world as his Father's world. He did not think of the natural order or cosmic forces apart from God. Neither did his Jewish contemporaries. They discussed God's rule. The question as to whether the universe is friendly to man was answered affirmatively by Jesus, as appears in his thought regarding God's manner of rule. Jesus looked upon the world order as purposive. God has a purpose, both in the order of nature, and in the order of history, and this purpose is beneficent. He is a God of love and holiness, who gives good things to men.[63] The Old Testament basis for such a view is:

I will make all my goodness pass before thee, and will proclaim the name of Yahweh before thee; and I will be gracious to whom I will be gracious, and will show mercy on whom I will show mercy.[64]

And Yahweh passed by before him, and proclaimed, Yahweh, Yahweh, a God merciful and gracious, slow to anger, and abundant in lovingkindness and truth; keeping lovingkindness for thousands, forgiving iniquity and transgression and sin.[65]

Jesus was a lover of nature and he looked to the on-goings of nature for evidence of God's manner of rule. In nature he found the benevolence of God manifested. The sun shines alike on the evil and the good; the rain falls upon the just and the unjust.[66] To Jesus this was evidence of God's love and care for all. For all the blessings that sunshine brings to him the good man believes that he is living in a friendly world. The evil man also finds that he is living in a friendly world because, despite his evil, the blessings of sunshine come to him. Both men alike are the sons of God in the sense that God takes the same Fatherly care of both. God's Fatherhood, in the view of Jesus, was primarily something not legal. He does not deal with his sons as they deserve, but better than they deserve.

"The earth beareth fruit of herself."[67] Jesus' observation and reflection upon human experience in the natural world makes him believe that the universe is friendly. The parable of the patient farmer is a parable of the kingdom of God.

And he said, So is the kingdom of God, as if a man should cast seed upon the earth; and should sleep and rise night and day, and the seed should spring up and grow, he knoweth not how. The earth beareth fruit of herself; first the blade, then the ear, then the full grain in the ear. But when the fruit is ripe, straightway he putteth forth the sickle, because the harvest is come.[68]

Nature's hidden forces are strong and good. Granted man's co-operation in plowing and sowing, these forces work for man's good. Good men and bad men alike sow the ground, go about their daily routine, and in due time reap a harvest of grain which nourishes them. Man does live in a friendly world. Jesus is concerned to say that the kingdom of God is like that, for that is the way God rules. Jesus affirms that God is ruling the world now. God is a *living* God, present and active. His manner of rule is Fatherly. The kingdom of God and the Fatherhood of God stand together in the thinking of Jesus.

Jesus looked not only to outward nature for evidence of God's manner of rule, but also to human nature. He observed a certain idealism in human nature which he made a basis for illustrating his conception of the ultimate reality. Consider the following:

Ask, and it shall be given you; seek, and ye shall find; knock, and it shall be opened unto you; for every one that asketh receiveth; and he that seeketh findeth; and to him that knocketh it shall be opened. Or what man is there of you, who, if his son shall ask him for a loaf, will give him a stone; or if he shall ask for a fish, will give him a serpent? If ye then, being evil, know how to give good gifts unto your children, how much more shall your Father who is in heaven give good things to them that ask him?[69]

Akin to this in idealism is the petition in the Lord's Prayer, as stated by Luke: "Forgive us our sins; for we ourselves also forgive every one that is indebted to us."[70] God cannot be less than man at his best is, and man at his best does find the spirit of forgiveness in his heart. We have previously quoted the splendid statement about forgiveness from the Testament of Gad.[71] Such idealism actually is in human nature. Its reality in no wise depends upon numerical preponderance. It is a solid fact of human experience. That he took this fact as his cue to an understanding of God's attitude toward men and the world shows how realistic Jesus was in his thinking. He had his feet on the ground.

Certainly a universe so constituted that the one who seeks finds, that the one who asks receives, is a friendly universe. Man himself with all his limitations and imperfections knows how to give good gifts and does give good gifts to his children. To Jesus this is but illustrative of God's Fatherhood, of God's manner of dealing with men. He gives good things to them that ask him. This principle is included in the petition: "Give us day by day our daily bread."[72]

Jesus threw further light on this principle in the parable of the vineyard owner and workers.[73] The full point of the parable is in the saying, "It is my will to give."[74] He here teaches that God freely gives his blessings to men according to their need. Salvation is a gift from God, not something earned. God is not put under obligation to man by anything that man does. The Father of mankind bestows his love and care as an ideal father would upon his children. The man in the parable paid what he promised to those he promised and gave what he pleased to those to whom he made no specific promise. His gracious action arose out of no merit of the recipients. There was no perversion of justice. So God does more than justice requires, he gives more than is deserved. Jesus is concerned to say that men live in a world like that, a friendly world.

The parable of the sower discloses the same thought in the mind of Jesus.[75] The sower scatters seed widely, not apportioning it according to the merit of the soil, confident that more will grow than will go to waste, for more of the soil is good than bad. This is further illustrative of God's generous, free, abounding, fatherly manner of dealing with men.

In such a world there is no occasion for anxiety.[76] The world is friendly to the birds of the heaven; "they sow not, neither do they reap, nor gather into barns; and your heavenly Father feedeth them."[77] They simply live out their own nature and find that the world is adjusted to the satisfaction of their needs. So the lilies of the field live out their own nature, neither toiling nor spinning, and God clothes them with beauty, and that is the object of their existence. In like manner man can in confident trust live out his own nature, not anxious about food or clothing or any such thing, for "your heavenly Father knoweth that ye have need of all these things."[78] Granted man's right religious adjustment, "Seek ye first his kingdom and his righteousness,"[79] man finds his world friendly: "all these things shall be added unto you."

Granted the right religious adjustment, the right attitude toward God, man finds the universe friendly to him. This religious attitude is faith. An attitude being a tendency to act toward an object, faith in God is a tendency to act with reference to God, to act in co-operation with the silent forces by which God works. The parables just cited are all parables of faith. The patient farmer actively co-operates with the unseen energies of nature by plowing the land and scattering the seed. That is his faith. He cannot force the appearance of the fruit. Having done all that is humanly possible in co-operating, he can do nothing more but wait. The harvest he regards as something given by God. The workers in the vineyard had faith in the owner that he would give them what was right and they went to work. The essence of faith is such co-operation. "Indeed, what attitude but one of reverence, sympathy, affection, and obedient co-operation can the reasonable and good man assume toward a friendly universe?"[80]

This principle in Jesus' world-view he based upon the Old Testament story of Jonah. The saying concerning "the sign of Jonah" occurs twice in Matthew and but once in Luke. Its basic form is in Matt. 16:4, "An evil and adulterous generation seeketh after a sign: and there shall no sign be given unto it, but the sign of Jonah;" there is no added explanation or expansion of the saying. In the other Matthean passage,[81] the logion is overlaid with later interpretation which relates the saying to the "Son of Man" being "three days and three nights in the heart of the earth." The Lukan parallel to this omits any reference to the three days and three nights and simply says, "Even as Jonah became a sign unto the Ninevites, so shall the Son of man be to this generation."[82] Taken in its basic form the saying simply means that Jonah is a sufficient sign of God at work in the world. In the Jonah story it was God who took the initiative in extending the benefits of his love to the (from the Jews' standpoint) undeserving Ninevites by sending Jonah to preach repentance to them. It is a clear and forceful picture of God acting. That is exactly the same kind of attitude on God's part toward man which Jesus set forth, a redeeming love which actively seeks man. The Ninevites repented under the stimulus of Jonah's preaching.

This truth is illustrated in the parable of the lost son.[83] It is a human story, right out of life, illustrating a certain disposition in man (the father of the prodigal), which disposition Jesus found in God also. It is a picture of the way fathers act. That is what the parable is for, to show what fatherhood is. Neither of the brothers is the central figure. The elder brother reflects one aspect of human nature in that he stopped at the justice of the procedure. The father, however, reflects another quality of human nature, and human nature at its highest responds to the principle of the care for the lost which is exhibited in the verses, unique for their insight:

While he was yet afar off, his father saw him, and was moved with compassion, and ran and fell on his neck, and kissed him.[84]

It was meet to make merry and be glad: for this thy brother was dead, and is alive again; and was lost and is found.[85]

The father's attitude was not determined by any principle of desert. The prodigal received a treatment he did not deserve and did not expect. The father was right; he did the most human thing. By his forbearance he did not close the way to his son's restoration to right living. Jesus means to say that God is forbearing and forgiving toward men. Here again Jesus takes the innate idealism of human nature as his cue to an understanding of God.

Jesus did not hold his world-view apart from his own practical attitude. His practical attitude is revealed in the setting in which Luke has put his parable of the lost son. Publicans and sinners are represented as drawing near to hear Jesus, and the Pharisees and scribes as complaining because "this man receiveth sinners and eateth with them."[86] What made the problem acute was the attitude of the Pharisees. They stopped with the discovery of sin, and thereafter avoided the sinner. The multitude of the common people were considered sinners. The benefits of religion were not for them, as these official representatives of religion declared it. Jesus did not stop with the discovery of sin. God's purpose was salvation, and that salvation reached to the needy in society. Through forbearance and forgiveness all men may be redeemed. To the question whether the world is friendly Jesus answered in effect: It is the heavenly Father's world, and he is good. Jesus' world-view expressed a lofty religious idealism, a lofty moral optimism.

Chapter V

EVIL

THE fact of evil presents the knottiest problem to human thought. It always has been so. It was so in Jesus' time. How sin was to be overcome in man and evil removed from the world was one of the chief elements in Jesus' teaching. Sin and evil were present in the experience of the people of Jesus' day no less than in our own time. In certain of its aspects, the problem of evil then too was acutely felt. Jesus knew the reality of evil. His problem, as a teacher of religion and ethics, was always the removal of evil, not its denial.

The problem of the origin of the natural world was, as has been pointed out, one of the chief interests of the Jewish thinkers, but it nowhere appears that they were concerned about incompleteness or imperfections in the natural order. The epic of creation in Genesis, chap. 1, declares: "God saw everything that he had made and, behold, it was very good."[1] With this view their minds seem to have rested. Jesus had such a view of nature. The God who cares for the lilies of the field[2] is the ruler of the earth. He made all things good. Omnipotence was one of the attributes of God emphasized in the Jewish literature of the New Testament period.[3]

Jesus' view of the natural order as good is reflected in the parables by which he illustrated the kingdom of God. The point of significance in the parable of the patient farmer[4] is that there is an omnipotent power silently at work which the farmer trusts because it works for his good. Implicit in the parable of the sower[5] is the problem of evil in nature. The ground is not all equally receptive. The fault is not with the sower or with the seed but with the soil. This was a real evil in the agriculture of Palestine. After a farmer's arduous labor had prepared and planted the soil, the grain might be taken by the birds, or blasted by the sun, or choked by weeds. What wonder that a man grew anxious about what he should eat on the morrow. That particular problem of anxiety Jesus dealt with as a religious problem—men may and must trust to God's providence. These unfavorable qualities of the soil do not, however, thwart the essentially good power of nature, for the earth does bear fruit of itself. Because God's created world is under his control, its ways are strong and good.

What Jesus thus observed in the physical world he applied to illustrate a truth of the spiritual realm. It is distinctive of Jesus to look on the inward side of things, discerning the hand of God in things spiritual and eternal rather than in things outward and spectacular. The parables of the mustard seed, the leaven, the patient farmer, and the sower illustrate the present, inward working of God's Spirit, a kingdom of God which is already in the midst, and though invisible, is invincible.[6]

Man did suffer from adverse elements in nature.[7] Jesus could cite such experiences, for evil in outward nature reflects man's nature and teaches him. The rains descended and the floods came and the winds blew and the house built upon the sand fell.[8] Such experience of adversity teaches man wisdom. It is not an irremediable evil. The fault was not with the storm but with the man. A man should build his house upon the rock. Jesus speaks of "eighteen upon whom the tower in Siloam fell and killed them."[9] A physical disaster of this sort was interpreted homiletically by Jewish teachers of religion as a punishment for man's sins. But to Jesus it did not argue that they were sinners above all others.

What about the good man when in peril? Will God miraculously deliver him? "He shall give his angels charge concerning thee: and, On their hands they shall bear thee up, lest haply thou dash thy foot against a stone."[10] Jesus faced this problem in the second temptation. Man, he believed, is not to presume upon God's love and power, but one can go his way in fearless trust, confident that no absolute or final disaster can befall him who seeks first God's kingdom.

Another phase of the problem of evil concerned the unmerited suffering of the righteous. The ancient Hebrews thought that God gave prosperity to the righteous and adversity to the wicked. It seemed reasonable that God would thus reward the good and punish the bad. The accepted doctrine of Judaism was that the measure of what was his due was meted out to the individual in this life; and therefore the outward lot of an individual was an infallible index to his character and his condition before God.

Writers of the Jewish literature felt keenly the problem of the suffering individual. Some explanation was found in the disciplinary value of suffering.[11] Sira makes temptation a test of a man's character.[12] Such considerations rest upon the principle of retribution in this life. The next step in this line of reasoning was to push the solution farther along and declare that a man's character is disclosed in the fate of his children.[13] Sira suggests that even on the day of a man's death God could still make right any inequities.[14]

The book of Job makes a great effort to account for the suffering of the righteous. The book is really an attack upon the accepted doctrine. Strangely enough, the book of Job as it stands is self-contradictory. In the prose part of the story, at the beginning and at the end, the righteous Job suffers in patience, so that God rewards him with greater riches. That is but to confirm the accepted view. In the poem, however, which constitutes the main portion of the book, Job is not patient. Although Job is faithfully religious, God is angry and sends suffering. Job cannot understand or reconcile this with the doctrine of divine rewards. The poet accepts the idea that suffering is disciplinary. Job had sinned in his self-righteousness.[15] He had to be cleansed of this through his suffering, against which he naturally protested. In the end, the poem portrays God as simply humbling Job by his divine greatness, and challenging Job to know anything about him and to question why he should expect anything from God. Regardless of appearances, Job was to trust him absolutely. The book of Job does not solve the problem of suffering; but it does show the fallacy of the conventional ideas.

Koheleth found a solution for this problem only in submission to an inevitable and unchanging order and in enjoying things as they come. His doctrine of God is a doctrine of determinism. Protest against the order of the universe is of no avail.[16] Submission is the prime virtue in such an order. One is to enjoy what comes.[17] In this pleasure one should exercise moderation and prudence, for excess brings evil. In cases of excess, sorrow is better than joy.[18]

The Psalms reveal the piety of Israel wrestling with the problem of evil and suffering. Many of the psalms are cries of distress. The proud and the wicked stand over against the righteous.[19] The nation suffers under the oppression of foreign powers. The psalms breathe, however, an ardent faith and a confidence that the future will vindicate the faith of the present. This appeal to the future is not to a future life after death, but to a redemption which man expects to experience in this life.

If the problem of the suffering of the righteous individual cannot be solved by appeal to the facts of experience, then the next logical step is to solve it by an appeal to a future life. Such an idea, however, did not find a congenial soil in Palestinian Judaism. Koheleth rejected it as an idle speculation.[20] He does not find any moral significance in life, for he has no ideal for either present or future. The fool and the wise man, the good man and the bad, all come to the same end and "all is futility." Such an outlook upon life is pessimism.

The assumption that outward material prosperity is evidence of inward righteousness Jesus denied outright. The question was concretely before him in the incident of the rich young ruler.[21] When Jesus counseled him to go sell whatever he had and give to the poor, "his countenance fell at the saying, and he went away sor-

rowful: for he was one that had great possessions."[22]
His great possessions were, on the accepted view, the
surest indication he had of God's satisfaction with him.
To give it all up and share the lot of the poor was to
him not only economically but religiously undesirable.
Jesus' comment on the incident was: "How hardly shall
they that have riches enter into the kingdom of God!
. . . It is easier for a camel to go through a needle's
eye, than for a rich man to enter into the kingdom of
God."[23] His disciples were "astonished exceedingly,"
for in the common view the man's very riches were interpreted as evidence that he was near to the kingdom
of God. In Jesus' thinking, riches constitute a spiritual
peril, and in much of his teaching he deals with the
right attitude toward material things.[24]

On the other hand, Jesus delivered the poor from the
depressing notion that because poor they were the objects of God's disfavor.[25] Luke represents that Jesus,
in the synagogue at Nazareth, read as an interpretation
of his own ministry the words of Isaiah 61:1, "The
Spirit of the Lord is upon me, because he anointed me
to preach good tidings to the poor."[26] Again, in response
to the inquiry of John the Baptist made through John's
disciples, Jesus called attention to the results attending
his ministry, among which was the fact that "The poor
have good tidings preached to them."[27] Indeed, Luke
gives the first beatitude simply as "Blessed are ye poor;

for yours is the kingdom of God."[28] All of this shows Jesus' sense of mutuality with plain people.

Further, Jesus solved this problem of the unmerited suffering of the righteous by teaching the heroic attitude which the righteous man may and should take toward life and toward the universe. This attitude may be termed *moral optimism*.[29]

This problem of unmerited suffering concerned the individual not only, but the nation. However history has judged the merits of the case, the Jews themselves felt that the Roman domination was an unmerited affliction. Some were for solving the problem by appeal to the sword. The Zealots stood for revolution. The party of the Pharisees, however, rather regarded the loss of national liberty as a penalty for the Jews' failure to keep the law and therefore the nation's chief business was to devote itself to the keeping of the law. Added to this was the apocalyptic hope. When the law was perfectly kept, Messiah would come, and the evil of foreign domination would be ended. This apocalyptic hope always glowed in times of oppression. It was a time of national oppression, the Maccabean period, which gave birth to this type of literature. It evidences profound faith in the power that makes for righteousness, for it asserts that God will, at a crucial time, assert himself in humanity.

Jesus largely shared this attitude of the Pharisees. He

nowhere concerns himself with politics, but everywhere with summoning the Jews, both as individuals, and as a nation, to a new righteousness. Jesus was not a legalist, but the ethical and religious ideals of the law he regarded as valid.[30] He likewise shared the apocalyptic hope, which we shall consider more fully in the next chapter.

The problem of moral evil, i. e., of the origin of sin, was the one problem on which Jewish thought became speculative. There were current in Jesus' time three theories as to how sin came into the world, which we may denominate the historical, the psychological, and the mythological theories.

The historical explanation was based upon the narrative of Adam and Eve and the Fall.[31] This narrative, basal in Jewish thinking and taken as literal fact, was interpreted as showing why the present age was sinful and needed to be destroyed. This explanation is used in II Baruch and IV Ezra, writings which, though dated after Jesus' time, reflect the current views of his time.

For though Adam first sinned
And brought untimely death upon all,
Yet of those who were born from him
Each one of them has prepared for his own soul torment
    to come
And again each one of them has chosen for himself glories
    to come.[32]

For the first Adam, clothing himself with the evil heart, transgressed and was overcome; and likewise also all who were born of him.[33]

For a grain of evil seed was sown in the heart of Adam from the beginning; and how much fruit of ungodliness has it produced to this time, and shall yet produce until the threshing-floor come![34]

Nowhere in the gospels is Jesus reported to have made reference to Adam and Eve. He did, however, accept the standard Jewish view that all men are sinners. This view was back of Jesus' reference to his hearers as "Ye that are evil;"[35] and his castigation of his age as a "faithless and perverse, evil and adulterous generation."[36] "For from within, out of the heart of men, evil thoughts proceed, fornications, thefts, murders, adulteries, covetings, wickednesses, deceit, lasciviousness, an evil eye, railing, pride, foolishness: all these evil things proceed from within."[37] Though like John the Baptist he called upon men to repent, he went beyond John's exhortation to "bring forth fruits worthy of repentance,"[38] in his remark: "When ye shall have done all the things that are commanded you, say, We are unprofitable servants."[39]

The psychological explanation attributes sin to man's evil heart, *yetser hara.*

> God created man from the beginning,
> And placed him in the hand of his *yetser*.[40]

The later rabbinical doctrine of the *yetser* is, according to F. C. Porter,[41] an elaboration of the doctrine thus expressed by Sira as to the source of sin in man. As Porter points out, the *yetser hara* does not concern a particular part of man's nature but rather man as a whole in whom the evil tendency or disposition dominates. The term is often translated by "passion." It designates the evil disposition which as a matter of experience does exist in man and which it is man's moral obligation to control. These evil tendencies range from sensual passions through anger and pride to religious unbelief and idolatry.[42] Man has full moral freedom and is morally responsible and if he will his good impulses and inclinations may gain control.

This presence of the *yetser* in man was not thought to cancel man's power of choice. It is this power of choice which the wisdom writers stress. They regard folly as the contradictory of wisdom, and they instruct their "sons," i. e., their pupils, in the way of wisdom, for ignorance is the cause of folly. Having set wisdom before their pupils, they leave the latter to their own choice. "If thou (so) desirest thou canst keep the commandments."[43] The implication of this is that man is free to choose the law or not.[44]

The customary Jewish remedy for the evil impulse is the law which, when studied and observed, nullifies the power of the *yetser hara*. Such was the solution which Sira proposed:

He that keepeth the law becometh master of the intent thereof;
And the end of the fear of the Lord is wisdom.[45]

The will must not only be instructed in the law but be divinely reinforced if the evil *yetser* is to be mastered and life controlled for righteousness.[46] Thus prayer is a help. The struggle against this evil impulse is ceaseless, but men are sustained by the assurance that in the world to come the evil impulse does not exist and the powers and qualities of heaven alone will rule.

This theory of evil inherent in the inner nature of man affords a basis for understanding Jesus' thought. "For from within, out of the heart of men, evil thoughts proceed . . . all these evil things proceed from within, and defile the man."[47] Jesus is concerned not so much with the explanation of evil as with its cure. If the source of evil is in the inner nature of man, the cure of it must be directed to the inner nature; hence, Jesus' principle of inwardness in his ethical teaching,[48] which in typical wisdom style he rested upon human choice. The Sermon on the Mount is brought to a conclusion by the parable of the two housebuilders,[49] a keen and forceful putting of the basic importance of human choice.

The mythological explanation attributes moral evil to the abuse of free will by created beings, both angelic and human. The development of the concept of the transcendence of God tended to make him inaccessible to men by separating him more and more from the world. This led to the development of angelology, for intermediary beings were necessary if man were to have any relationship to God at all. The apocalyptic writers placed the beginnings of transgression in the angel world. According to Genesis 6:1-4, the relationship of the degenerate angels with the daughters of men brought evil on the earth. On the basis of this suggestion, the apocalyptists worked out an elaborate demonology as a solution of the problem of evil.[50] Demons were the spirits which proceeded forth from the souls of the giants born of the illicit union of the fallen angels with the daughters of men.[51] That such union with human beings should produce evil reflects the Persian conception of matter as essentially corrupt. Among these demons were Satan and Azazel. The Testaments of the Twelve Patriarchs and the Ascension of Isaiah portray the world as full of demonic spirits, the personification of men's evil inclinations, all under the headship of Beliar. We have a picture of the activity of a Persian demon, Asmodaeus, in the book of Tobit. Demons were conceived as working moral ruin unrestrained until their final judgment as disembodied spirits.

This thought-pattern underlies the synoptic gospels. The conception of demons as disembodied spirits is in Jesus' parable of the returning demon:

> But the unclean spirit, when he is gone out of the man, passeth through waterless places, seeking rest, and findeth it not. Then he saith, I will return into my house whence I came out; and when he is come, he findeth it empty, swept and garnished. Then goeth he, and taketh with himself seven other spirits more evil than himself, and they enter in and dwell there.[52]

The idea that the demons are not punished until the final judgment is reflected in the cry of the Gadarene demoniac, "Art thou come hither to torment us before the time?"[53]

Among the incidents of healing disease attributed to Jesus in the synoptic gospels, certain cases are commonly designated the casting out of demons.[54] Man was believed to be constantly acted upon in hurtful fashion by demons which were thought to enter into man's body and displace his normal consciousness. Exorcism was the method of cure.[55] The ordinary exorcist used such means as the liver of a fish, or the name of an angel, or a mysterious formula, or the like.[56] The beneficial effect came through the patient's faith in the means employed. Jesus did not use magical means.

He simply commanded the demons to depart. Mere exorcism did not effect permanent cure.[57] Jesus put a new idea into the demoniac's mind and that was sufficient expulsive power. On Matthew's representation, it was "by the Spirit of God" that Jesus cast out demons.[58] The Spirit of God displaced the expelled spirit and that made the cure permanent. Jesus believed that God's power was sufficient and simply needed to be appealed to by stimulating the sufferer's faith in it. Men did fear the demons and this was the real evil. Jesus did not believe that there was any other superhuman being than God whom men need trust or fear. This is not to say that Jesus did not believe in the existence of demons. He probably did, but he certainly did deny their power and deliver men from their power. He had the clear insight to see that it was inconsistent with Israel's creed, "God is one,"[59] to believe in the power of demons and to fear that power, especially when such demons were regarded as the agents of a lord demon under whose charge the world was assumed to be.

Jewish thinking in Jesus' time was dualistic. They of course believed in God, but Satan was regarded as the ruler of the present age. Jesus was no dualist, but a consistent monotheist. His teaching recalled Judaism to monotheism. This aspect of Jesus' world-view is manifest in the Beelzebub discourse.[60] Jesus was charged by his foes with being in alliance with Beelzebub, the prince of demons.[61] That is, they charged that his power came from an evil source. Jesus pointed out that such a charge meant that Satan was divided against himself, and they did not believe that Satan's interest, as prince of demons, would be to cast out demons, but rather to cast them into people. The more who became demon-possessed, the more would Satan's kingdom spread. But the opposite was proving to be the case in Jesus' ministry.

Jesus added, "But if I by the Spirit[62] of God cast out demons, then is the kingdom of God come upon you."[63] The power which does good is God's power. It is not right to attribute a good deed to Satan, and even Jesus' enemies considered exorcism a good deed, for their "sons" practiced it.[64] Jesus was against Satan and with God. The fact that such a good work could prevail was, in Jesus' view, proof that the power of God is present to co-operate with man in the deliverance from evil. Jesus' view was that the present world belongs to God, for his prevailing power is at hand. However much Jesus expressed himself in terms of Satan and demons, he did not regard them as powers which offered any serious opposition to God. Jesus' concern was to defend monotheism against the denial of it.

How was sin to be removed in the present age? In the approved view of standard Judaism, by the keeping of the law. This was the ritual remedy, external and legalistic, for the ceremonial and the ethical in the law were not distinguished. Jesus did distinguish them, and placed the emphasis in his teaching on righteousness, not ritual.

Jesus did not discuss the problem of evil in the abstract. He set forth his views in simple stories out of life, thus grounding his world-view in actual common-sense experience. It is open to the simplest man to interrogate his experience and his environment. He has at hand all that he needs for shaping a philosophy of life. The parable of the wheat and the tares[65] implies that nature's forces are good and not evil. The farmer sowed wheat and trusted the earth for a harvest. It was an enemy that sowed the tares, i. e., the perverse wilfulness of man directed nature's forces for evil ends. The evil will of men is the real evil in the world. Growing together in the same field, the tares were a challenge to the supremacy of the wheat and to the purposes which the wheat served. But at the final reckoning in the day of harvest, the wheat triumphs. The tares are not burned just to get rid of them. The economy of living in Palestine forbade any such waste. Tares are bound in bundles for fuel and when so used they serve the real purpose of the wheat by assisting the baking of the bread. This is a parable of faith in the supremacy of good and its ultimate triumph, as well as a parable of non-resistance. "Resist not evil,"[66] is Jesus' fundamental dictum. Such forbearance of evil on God's part is not a sign of his incapacity, nor of his indifference. By forbearance of evil, evil is overcome. The parable of the lost son[67] illustrates love in forbearance with the evil man, another example of non-resistance in operation.

Jesus practised non-resistance in his own ministry, as evidenced by his association with the religiously neglected publicans, sinners, and the diseased. "Sinners were drawing near unto him to hear him."[68] Apropos of this statement, Montefiore writes:

> This verse sums up one of the specific characteristics of Jesus and one of the new excellences of the gospel. . . . Surely this is a new note, something which we have not yet heard in the Old Testament or of *its* heroes, something which we do not hear in the Talmud or of *its* heroes. . . . The virtues of repentance are gloriously praised in the rabbinical literature, but this direct search for, and appeal to, the sinner, are new and moving notes of high import and significance. The good shepherd who searches for the lost sheep, and reclaims it and rejoices over it, is a new figure, which has never ceased to play its great part in the moral and religious development of the world.[69]

Disease was looked upon as punishment for sin, the diseased person being *ipso facto* a sinful person. Montefiore states:

> It must be admitted that the theory that suffering or disease implied sin was the prevailing rabbinic doctrine, at

all events in the later centuries. One rabbi states categorically (R. Ammi, about A.D. 300) that there is no death without guilt, no (bodily) suffering without sin. And another, R. Alexandrai (same date) declares that no man gets up from his sickness till God has forgiven all his sins.[70]

Concerning Jesus' attitude toward such sufferers, who were despised by their fellow men and believed themselves despised and rejected by God, Montefiore finds that "Here is a new and lofty note, a new and exquisite manifestation of the very pity and love which the prophets had demanded."[71] This lofty note is that of love in forbearance.

Jesus in his own living identified himself with truth as he saw the truth. He found in Second Isaiah the principle that the building of righteousness is founded on suffering that is vicarious. Jesus foresaw for himself opposition and martyrdom, and for his disciples persecution. A first-century Christian writer said that Jesus "for the joy that was set before him endured the cross."[72] This is an appreciation of Jesus as one whose faith in the triumph of righteousness was such that he cheerfully identified himself with the cause of righteousness and took the consequences. Montefiore sees this in the right light:

Among those virtues upon which he laid stress may we not safely assume that the virtue of self-sacrifice, of service for the sake of others, was undoubtedly one. Is it not reasonable, then, to suppose that he looked upon his own life as a service, and that this thought may even have developed into the idea that he might have to die in order to complete his service? Death would not be the end; death was to no man the end; certainly not the righteous; least of all to the messiah. Was the glory and the triumph perhaps only to come *after* the life of service had been ended by a death of sacrifice? If the principle of non-resistance was adopted by him in his ethics for daily life, it is not unnatural that it should have been adopted by him as regards his own special life and his position as Messiah.[73]

This means that Jesus solved the problem of evil not so much theoretically as practically and vitally.

How was evil to be removed in the coming age? By its catastrophic overthrow through God's direct intervention. Such was the standard view of Judaism. This conception was not an eccentric or tangential feature of Jewish thinking, but was integrated with their philosophy of history. It was an adaptation of the theory applied to the original creation and the flood.

This conception is applied to the original creation by Second Isaiah:

Awake, awake, put on strength, O arm of Yahweh; awake, as in the days of old, the generations of ancient times. Is it not thou that didst cut Rahab in pieces, that didst pierce the monster?[74]

The reference here is to the ancient Hebrew myth of Yahweh's contest with Rahab the great dragon, who personified the primeval chaos.[75] By a mighty act of intervention Yahweh overcame the forces of chaos and established the cosmos. This theory of course rests back upon the Babylonian myth of Marduk's slaying of Tiamat, the Babylonian counterpart of Rahab, after which victory Marduk proceeded to create the world and man.[76] "The Babylonian myth gave the apocalyptists their philosophy of the universe."[77]

In Jewish thought, Yahweh similarly rose up at the time of the flood to destroy evil.

And Yahweh saw that the wickedness of man was great in the earth, and that every imagination of the thoughts of his heart was only evil continually.

And Yahweh said, I will destroy man whom I have created from the face of the ground.[78]

That this theory had an important place in Jewish thinking in Jesus' time is seen in the fact that the Similitudes of Enoch (I Enoch 37-71), dated by Charles either 94-79 or 70-64 B.C.,[79] expounds this view of the first world judgment in several Noachic fragments which deal mainly with the Deluge.[80]

"Eschatology is the natural corollary of cosmogony."[81] Jewish eschatology applied this same philosophy of history to the future and declared that once again God would rise and by a mighty act of intervention overthrow the forces of evil and inaugurate a new age of righteousness. This is a conventional item in the general Jewish program of eschatological events. Zechariah 14 presents a vivid picture of Yahweh's irruption into the existing order to overthrow evil and establish righteousness. This conventional idea appears to have been Jesus' view also. It is definitely ascribed to him in the apocalyptic discourses in Matthew and Luke. "And as it came to pass in the days of Noah, even so shall it be also in the days of the Son of man." [82] The climax of evil is followed by the great cataclysm in which evil is overthrown.[83]

This theory is not inconsistent with what we have observed in previous chapters regarding Jesus' world-view. He thought of God as a Father whose character is love and whose purpose is salvation, in view of which purpose he is forbearing with evil. Men may however deliberately choose to continue in sin. What then? "The only absolute disaster to be feared is to be found in continued sin and its necessary personal and social consequences."[84] Jesus saw this possibility and unhesitatingly taught the consequences. This is illustrated in the parable of the lord's vineyard, found in all three synoptic gospels.[85] Here is a picture of deliberate and willful evil behavior. In the end, after all other means had been exhausted, there was nothing for the lord of the vineyard to do but to come and destroy the husbandmen and give the vineyard to others.

This doctrine was not only ethically based, but it

functioned ethically. This portrayal of the ultimate destruction of evil was used by Jesus, as well as by other Jewish teachers of religion and ethics, as a powerful incentive for doing right. Certainly this hope that righteousness soon would triumph and that all sin and evil would be forever banished, kept the Jewish people from despair in times of suffering under oppression, and was an urge to self-sacrifice and heroic endeavor. So it was also to the primitive Christians.

A modern philosopher states the matter, not on the ground of New Testament teaching, but on the ground of inherent reasonableness, as follows:

There can be satisfaction of the moral, Christlike God only in the destruction of sin and its evil consequences. Full satisfaction of God's righteousness belongs therefore to the future rather than to the past. . . . It is only as the triumph of good over evil either is being experienced or is anticipated in faith that there can be any true satisfaction of righteousness, human or divine.[86]

Jesus did in his world-view anticipate the complete removal of evil from man and the world. Of course God will ultimately overthrow evil, for God is at present an immanent force doing that very thing, which is what Jesus asserted in the Beelzebub discourse.[87]

Chapter VI

THE FUTURE

THE dominant emphasis of the great Old Testament prophets, beginning with the eighth century, B.C., was ethical. The prophets were pre-eminently men of profound ethical insight. The passion which characterized their preaching was inspired by their appreciation of ethical values. Their constructive ethical teaching was usually given in reaction against externalism in morals and ritualism in religion. Fearlessly they denounced unrighteous individuals and pronounced doom upon the sinful nation. Their condemnation of sin came about through their intense feeling for righteousness.[1]

The prophets were not primarily predictors of future events. They were concerned to proclaim the will of God who is the Eternal. They therefore dealt with past, present, and future.[2] In the past they saw what God had wrought, and this formed the basis of the principles which they set forth for the present. When they did make predictions concerning the future, their aim was to stimulate righteousness in the present. They proclaimed the coming doom of the sinful nation in order to stir the nation to present repentance. When they declared a hope of future restoration and blessing for the nation, it was a hope for a morally purged Israel, and the intent of such hope was that faith might not fail among those who in the present were upright. It was, therefore, under the inspiration of their own religious faith that they made forecasts of the future. If these forecasts failed, the prophets were not deterred. They went on declaring the will of God.

Two aspects of prophecy are therefore discernible, the one relating to right conduct in the present, the other being concerned with the issues of the future. These two phases are termed wisdom and eschatology.

Contemporaneous with the Old Testament prophets were the professional wise men. This wisdom type of study and teaching represented the line of general education. Jewish education was religious education. It concerned itself with the same ethical values which the prophets stressed. Thus wisdom came to be the best type of prophetic activity. After the period of prophecy was thought formally to have closed, the ethical impulse of prophecy continued to find expression in the teaching of wisdom. Wisdom teaching carried forward the teaching work of prophecy continuously down to 100 A.D. It is among these wisdom teachers that we have classified Jesus.[3] The great Hebrew prophets were outstanding personalities. Few of the wisdom teachers were such. Jesus was a striking personality. He revived the best traits and activities of the older prophetic type and for that reason he was rated as a prophet.[4] Paul was, in part, a wisdom teacher. The book of James is evidence that Christianity carried forward this wisdom interest.

In the wisdom literature, therefore, the dominant emphasis is ethical. The wisdom teachers, however, did not neglect eschatology. They gave it attention because it completed their ideal of righteousness and because it functioned ethically as an incentive to righteousness. This is illustrated in three distinctly wisdom books, Sira and the Testaments of the Twelve Patriarchs, belonging to the second century, B.C., and the Book of Wisdom, belonging to the first century, B.C. Sira anticipated a messianic kingdom,[5] of which Elijah was to be the forerunner.[6] Israel was to be delivered from evil,[7] the scattered tribes brought back,[8] and the heathen punished.[9] The Testaments express the hope of a messiah,[10] and have much to say about his character and functions.[11] There is to be a resurrection,[12] and a future kingdom on earth. The Book of Wisdom expects a messianic kingdom,[13] and sets forth at some length a doctrine of the resurrection,[14] and of the future punishment of the wicked.[15] Thus we observe that eschatological teaching is present as an essential factor in the wisdom teaching.[16] It is, however, subordinated to the ethical teaching, which it is designed to emphasize and enforce. No more conspicuous example of the combining of wisdom teaching with apocalyptic can be cited than II Enoch. Chapters 1-41 are very speculative and fantastic. Chapters 42-66 are dominantly ethical teaching and present many noble sentiments, abundant use being made of the beatitude form of teaching.[17]

The Old Testament prophetic books contain an eschatological element. The prophets portrayed a glorious future which would see the sifting of Israel, all present evils eradicated, and the interests and activities of the present world purified and heightened. They were not mere visionaries, but related the future organically and ethically to the present. The predictive aspect of the prophecy of the early period was carried forward by apocalyptic. In fact it was the re-editing of unfulfilled prophecy which gave rise to apocalyptic. Ezekiel is credited with being one of the spiritual founders of apocalyptic,[18] because of his re-vamping of the unfulfilled predictions of Jeremiah,[19] and Zephaniah,[20] regarding the invasion of Judah from the north by a mighty foe, into his speculative invasion of Palestine by Gog from the land of Magog. "Art thou he of whom I spake in old time by my servants the prophets of Israel, that prophesied in those days for many years that I would bring thee against them?"[21] Prophecy and apocalyptic are not mutually opposed; they have a common

basis, they use prevailingly the same methods, and both
are fundamentally ethical.

Apocalyptic is mainly eschatology, but not exclusively. It reaches back sometimes in its thought to find a
plan of God running through history. Thus Daniel
deals with the present or the immediate past;[22] I Enoch
deals with all the past preceding the life of Enoch;[23] II
Baruch deals with the leading crises in the world's history down to Baruch's time;[24] the Sibylline Oracles give
an account of the beginnings of history down to the
Deluge.[25] The cosmic purpose and plan of God, especially as it concerns the destiny of man and the world,
is brought under survey in apocalyptic.

The apocalyptist sought to get behind the surface and
penetrate to the essence of events, the spiritual purposes and
forces that underlie and give them their real significance.
With this end in view apocalyptic sketched in outline the
history of the world and of mankind, the origin of evil, its
course, and inevitable overthrow, the ultimate triumph of
righteousness, and the final consummation of all things. It
was thus, in short, *a Semitic philosophy of religion,* and as
such it was ever asking, Whence? Wherefore? Whither?
and it put these questions in connection with the world,
the Gentiles, Israel, and the individual. Apocalyptic and not
prophecy was the first to grasp the great idea that all history, alike human, cosmological, and spiritual, is a unity—a
unity following naturally as a corollary of the unity of God
preached by the prophets.[26]

To use our own terminology, apocalyptic was essentially a world-view, and as such it was established upon a basis of ethical idealism. The essence of that ethical idealism was the righteousness of God. Convinced that the Judge of all the earth would do right, apocalyptic as a world-view was at all times morally optimistic and answered the challenge of every crisis when evil overpowered good by asserting that ultimately righteousness will prevail.[27] Such a philosophy, cosmic in its range, represents an advanced stage of ethical reflection and is therefore a late development of Jewish thinking.[28] Apocalyptic believes in and anticipates the attainment of ethical ideals, of the ideal humanity.

While thus characterizing apocalyptic as a world-view, as a philosophy of religion, Deissmann's appraisal of it is accurate:

We are not concerned here with a closely knit body of thought worked out and built up from the quiet speculation of the schools, but with the impressionist pictures of the future, rich and joyful in color, mostly related to one another in style, by unknown masters of popular art, whose meaning is to be grasped by a single glance without long searching. All these pictures say, in antique oriental Jewish colors not seldom with exaggerations into the grotesque, miraculous, fantastic, and horrible, what the most genuine of genuine piety is: they testify the certainty that God is present, God is active, God rescues, God redeems.[29]

This picture-thinking character of eschatology Wilder calls myth.

But whereas most myth represents the unknown past and gives a symbolic picture of unknown origins, eschatology is that form of myth which represents the unknown future.[30]

In modern times we distinguish between prophecy and apocalypse. The ancient Jewish writers did not. They knew it all as prophecy. The term apocalypse was introduced by Greek-speaking Christians. The book of Revelation, e. g., designated an apocalypse by the very first word in it, none the less calls itself a "book of prophecy."[31] The apocalyptists were the prophets of their day.

Post-exilic Judaism developed on the one hand a severe legalism which tended to suppress religious enthusiasm and mystical faith, as well as ethical spontaneity. This legalism appealed to a certain type of the scribes who concerned themselves with codifying, interpreting, and expounding the law. Others were not of this attitude of mind, and with them ethical and educational zeal sought a different outlet for their religious faith and they found it in wisdom and apocalyptic, which developed the more spiritual Judaism. Legalism and apocalyptic were not essentially antagonistic in pre-Christian times. Both started from the law. The Testaments of the Twelve Patriarchs declare that the light of the law was given to lighten every man.[32] Both agreed on the validity of the prophetic teaching and the right of apocalyptic as its successor, as can be observed in Jubilees which, though "the narrowest book that ever was written by legalistic Judaism,"[33] yet included a large amount of apocalyptical material. In the book of Joel legalism and apocalyptic are joined.

The representatives of educational Judaism fall into two classes. With one class wisdom received the major emphasis and apocalyptic the minor, as pointed out in the foregoing. With the other class, apocalyptic received the major emphasis and wisdom the minor. This latter fact is illustrated in two writings, I and II Enoch. I Enoch 91-104 contains specific ethics. Much of the wisdom instruction here given is in the form of "woes" pronounced upon the wicked. The purpose of such warnings is to turn men to righteousness. Counsels of comfort for the righteous are likewise included. Thus eschatological speculation and ethical teaching are thoroughly integrated in one world-view. II Enoch similarly includes wisdom teaching with apocalyptic. Chapter 9 describes the righteous, chapter 10 the wicked, and from chapter 41 on the book is almost wholly made up of wisdom teaching, much of which is given in the form of "beatitudes."

On this basis of the ethical idealism inherent in both wisdom and apocalyptic is to be understood the place of eschatology in the world-view of Jesus. "An eschatological religion entails an ethic by maintaining a moral nexus between this life and the next."[34] Everything in Jesus' world-view pivots upon his ethical idealism. The question is not one of *either* ethics *or* eschatology. Both are there integrally in his thinking, according to the representation of all sources. He could not have presented an effective ethical message to his age if he had neglected the thought of the ultimate realization of ethical values.

Among modern interpreters of Jesus, anti-eschatologists incline to construe the eschatology as an element read back into the mind of Jesus by the ensuing generation of his followers. Jesus, they maintain, taught ethics, not eschatology. At the other extreme, some understand Jesus' eschatology as the all-important element in his thinking. On this view his ethics is secondary to his eschatology. That is to say, it was an interim ethics. Neither extreme is right. Jesus did not base his ethics upon his eschatology. He based his eschatology upon his ethics. His ethics is the basal thing in his world-view and his world-view did include eschatology.

The central value in Jewish eschatology is righteousness. Righteousness was the condition of entrance into the kingdom. The kingdom was to be a kingdom of righteousness. Inwardly Jesus felt a deep, intense appreciation of God and righteousness, a conviction of certainty that righteousness was and was to be supreme over evil. How could such an assurance find expression with a first-century Jew, if not in the thought-forms of his people and his age? He was bound to express himself in eschatological terms just as we in the twentieth century are bound to express ourselves in evolutionary thought-forms. The more intense the inner appreciation, the more vivid the outward expression. Hence the highly colored imagery of Jesus' eschatological discourses. Behind such imagery is the basic thing in the thinking of Jesus:—his inner appreciation of righteousness and assurance of its ultimate supremacy. E. F. Scott well says:

It must never be forgotten that the apocalyptic ideas, although they assumed a peculiar form in the later Judaism, were not merely the product of a bizarre movement. The hope for the kingdom of God had always been central to the religion of Israel. Out of the faith in the one righteous God there had inevitably sprung the belief that he would at last be sovereign over the whole world. Apocalyptic was nothing but the imaginative expression of this primary belief. It becomes evident, too, the more we study the thought of Jesus, that he used apocalyptic only as a sort of pictorial language. His message is in no way dependent on those fanciful conceptions, current in his time. It can be separated from them and thrown into other forms, without any loss of its intrinsic meaning.[35]

The ethics of Jesus is not an interim ethics. He is not

concerned to teach men how to live in an interval. His message is concerned with eternal life, i. e., with life in an eternal world-order. Weinel well says:

What follows for man from the coming of the divine world is alone of weight for Jesus. If God's rule comes—and it stands at the door—of what sort must the man be who can live under such a ruler? Are you such a man? That is the question which he puts to every single one of his people.[36]

We have a clear example of what interim ethics is like in Jeremiah:

The word of Yahweh came unto me, saying, Thou shalt not take thee a wife, neither shalt thou have sons or daughters, in this place. For thus saith Yahweh concerning the sons and concerning the daughters that are born in this place, and concerning their mothers that bare them, and concerning their fathers that begat them in this land: They shall die grievous deaths: they shall not be lamented, neither shall they be buried; they shall be as dung upon the face of the ground; and they shall be consumed by the sword, and by the famine; and their dead bodies shall be food for the birds of the heavens, and for the beasts of the earth.

For thus saith Yahweh, Enter not into the house of mourning, neither go to lament, neither bemoan them; for I have taken away my peace from this people, saith Yahweh, even lovingkindness and tender mercies. Both great and small shall die in this land; they shall not be buried, neither shall men lament for them, nor cut themselves, nor make themselves bald for them; neither shall men break bread for them in mourning, to comfort them for the dead; neither shall men give them the cup of consolation to drink for their father or for their mother. And thou shalt not go into the house of feasting to sit with them, to eat and to drink. For thus saith Yahweh of hosts, the God of Israel: Behold, I will cause to cease out of this place, before your eyes and in your days, the voice of mirth and the voice of gladness, the voice of the bridegroom and the voice of the bride.[37]

Here, plainly, everything for the prophet is determined by the impending catastrophe. What lies beyond that event is not taken into account as a basis for his present behavior. In striking contrast to such thinking is Jesus. He certainly did not practice or teach asceticism. His denunciation of hypocrisy,[38] and his counseling of love toward one's enemies,[39] are not made in view of an imminent catastrophe but in view of an ultimate, absolute, ethical demand that men may be sons of God.[40]

There was variety and freedom in Jewish eschatological thinking. With some writers it found expression in highly figurative and fanciful forms. Eschatological ideas were not systematized or dogmatized. There were, however, certain conventional items common to the various eschatological programs, viz., the last evils; the coming of the messiah; the overthrow of evil, including the renewing (purification) of the earth; the resurrection; the judgment; the eternal awards of punishment for the wicked and eternal life for the righteous.

Apocalyptical writers usually regard this world as a kingdom of evil, doomed to destruction. As the end draws near, Satan's power is exerted to increase the woes and sufferings of the people. History will terminate in the climax of evil. Such woes are vividly portrayed in Jubilees,[41] II Baruch,[42] and IV Ezra.[43] This feature of the conventional program of last things appears in the eschatological discourse chapters of the synoptic gospels.[44] It is implied, though not expressly stated, in Luke 17, the discourse on the coming of the kingdom, which is of considerable importance because separate from the so-called "little apocalypse."[45] In so far as Jesus incorporated this conception of the last evils in his world-view, it was as a conventional feature of Jewish thinking. It is not a subject he elaborated, or one in which his major interest lay.

In the messianic passages of the Old Testament, Kent distinguishes three types of messianic hope. First, the kingly and national hope anticipated a messiah who would be a conquering hero like David and would build up a world empire around Israel as a nucleus. This ideal appealed to popular patriot and statesman in earlier times, and was the hope of the common people and especially the Zealots in New Testament times. Second, the apocalyptic and catastrophic type of hope expects Yahweh himself to appear as a divine warrior and miraculously destroy the heathen powers and vindicate his people by setting them in the preferred place in the divine kingdom. In later Judaism the warrior conception of Yahweh seemed inconsistent with the transcendence of the deity and there developed the conception of an angelic messiah, one like unto a Son of Man, to come on the clouds to establish a kingdom of the righteous. This type of hope appealed to idealists and pietists in ancient Israel, and in Roman times to the Essenes and, to a large extent, the Pharisees. The third type of ideal, the ethical and universalistic, anticipated a kingdom in which God's will would be fully recognized and done.[46]

The Old Testament passages reveal a trace of the messiah idea prior to 200 B.C.[47] Messiah is regarded as an ideal king through whom God will achieve his purposes by endowing him with wisdom and power.

The apocryphal and apocalyptical literature of later Judaism discloses two types of messiah, the one human, the other transcendental. Whether human or transcendental, he is regarded as the divinely provided and appointed agent for bringing to pass the last things, chiefly the effective carrying out of God's purposes.[48] The pre-eminent quality in the character of the messiah is that he is righteous. It is this which guarantees his ability to carry out the righteous purposes of God.[49]

Equally significant is his wisdom. It is by this quality that he succeeds in his work of establishing righteousness.[50] I Enoch says of the transcendental messiah:

> Wisdom is poured out like water, and glory does not fail before him for evermore. . . . And in him dwells the spirit of wisdom . . . and the spirit of understanding and of might, and the spirit of those who have fallen asleep in righteousness.[51]

The Sibylline Oracles (200-100 B.C.) speak of Messiah coming from the east,[52] and in I Enoch 90 (200-100 B.C.) Messiah appears as a lamb and transforms the righteous into his likeness,[53] but in both of these, Messiah plays no part in the kingdom. I Enoch 37-71 terms the messiah the Christ,[54] the Righteous One,[55] the Elect One,[56] but most frequently the Son of Man.[57] In this work the Son of Man has the three functions of judge of the world, revealer of all things, and champion and ruler of the righteous.[58] Psalms of Solomon 17, 18 presents a militant messiah. In II Baruch, Messiah appears at the close of the messianic woes.[59] In IV Ezra, the messiah appears at the same time as the first resurrection;[60] the Son of Man comes on the clouds.[61] He is portrayed in II Baruch and IV Ezra as an active warrior who destroys his enemies by his own hand,[62] or by the word of his mouth.[63]

It is the conception of the transcendental Son of Man which alone is of importance to the world-view of Jesus.

It is attributed to Jesus in the "little apocalypse" in the synoptic gospels:

And then shall they see the Son of Man coming in clouds with great power and glory. And then shall he send forth the angels, and shall gather together his elect from the four winds, from the uttermost part of the earth to the uttermost part of heaven.[64]

More significantly still, this conception is found in an important passage not connected with the "little apocalypse." Replying to a question concerning the time of the Parousia, Jesus is reported as saying:

The days will come, when ye shall desire to see one of the days of the Son of Man, and ye shall not see it. . . . For as the lightning, when it lighteneth out of the one part under the heaven shineth unto the other part under heaven; so shall the Son of Man be in his day. . . . As it came to pass in the days of Noah, even so shall it be also in the days of the Son of Man.[65]

That Jesus should hold such a view is altogether likely in the light of the basic material discussed in the foregoing and in view of the other factors in his worldview. His world-view is thoroughly idealistic and is concerned with the achievement of the ideal humanity. This conception of the Son of Man is a conception of the ideal righteous person who will accomplish the ideal mission. Such a conception represented the "highest ascent of prophetism."[66] Moreover, the place of this conception in the world-view of Jesus is exactly the same whether Jesus thought of himself as this Son of Man or not. Into the moot question of Jesus' self-consciousness we are not obliged to go in this connection. We are here concerned only with the world-view of Jesus. In that world-view the character and function of this ideal Son of Man was what it was whatever his identity.[67]

Philosophically construed, apocalyptic asserts that *the world order is purposive*. The apocalyptic hope deals with the ultimate relations of God to the present world order, as well as to the individual person. Therefore an important item in the standard Jewish eschatological program was the intervention of God for the overthrow of evil, which has been discussed in Chapter V, and for the renewing (purification) of the earth. Upon the ruins of the old world a new order will rise. "This assurance that God will renew the world for the sake of Israel is the inspiring motive of all the apocalypses."[68] The new age is to be essentially good and eternal. The doctrine of the renewed earth is present in Isaiah 65, 66.

For, behold, I create new heavens and a new earth; and the former things shall not be remembered, nor come to mind. But be ye glad and rejoice for ever in that which I create; for, behold, I create Jerusalem a rejoicing, and her people a joy.[69]

For as the new heavens and the new earth, which I shall

make, shall remain before me, saith Yahweh, so shall your seed and your name remain.[70]

The thought here is of a gradual transformation, both in the nature of man and of the world as well. It is the same Jerusalem, only supernaturally transformed. Similarly Jubilees says:

Mount Zion will be sanctified in the new creation for a sanctification of the earth.[71]

In the apocalyptical writings dating from the beginning of the first century, B.C., the transformation of the earth is conceived as cataclysmic.

And the first heaven shall depart and pass away,
And a new heaven shall appear,
And all the powers of the heavens shall give sevenfold light.

And after that there will be many weeks without number for ever,
And all shall be in goodness and righteousness,
And sin shall no more be mentioned for ever.[72]

And I will transform the heaven and make it an eternal blessing and light:
And I will transform the earth and make it a blessing:

And I will cause mine elect ones to dwell upon it:
But the sinners and evil-doers shall not set foot thereon.[73]

In II Baruch "the Mighty One will renew his creation;"[74] the world becomes a "world which does not die,"[75] a "world to which there is no end;"[76] incorruptible,[77] and invisible.[78] This renewal of the earth is regarded as the fulfillment of the promises made to Abraham, in whose time "hope of the world that was to be renewed was then built up, and the promise of the life that should come hereafter was implanted."[79] The same thought of the eschatological renewal of the earth is present in IV Ezra,[80] II Peter,[81] and Revelation.[82]

Upon the arrival of this new order upon a divinely renewed earth the sufferings of the righteous are at an end. Those sufferings are thus seen to be a necessary link in the chain of events, due to the dominance of sin and evil in the present order of things. Here then is a new solution of the problem of evil.

It is this conception of a divinely renewed earth which is implied in Jesus' teaching: "Blessed are the meek, for they shall inherit the earth."[83] It also motivates the petition: "Thy will be done, as in heaven, so on earth."[84] It is likewise implied in the synoptic discourses, especially in the citation: "As it came to pass in the days of Noah, even so shall it be also in the days of the Son of Man."[85] In the days of Noah by divine intervention evil was destroyed and the earth was renewed.

The doctrine of the resurrection of the dead is prominent in the apocalyptical literature as one of the primary features of the eschatological program. This doctrine was clearly established and widely held in later Judaism, i. e., after 200 B.C. The doctrine varies with the different writers, some holding to the resurrection of the righteous only, others maintaining the resurrection of all alike, good and bad. The doctrine of a resurrection for all was a corollary of their doctrine of the day of judgment. All must arise from the dead in order to present themselves before God for judgment.

The earliest definite expressions of the idea of a resurrection are:

Thy dead shall live; my dead bodies shall arise. Awake and sing, ye that dwell in the dust; for thy dew is as the dew of herbs, and the earth shall cast forth the dead.[86]

And many of them that sleep in the dust of the earth shall awake, some to everlasting life, and some to shame and everlasting contempt.[87]

The origin of the former passage is variously dated from 334 B.C. to *ca.* 100 B.C.[88] and by some is interpreted as applying only to the righteous, in view of the emphasis in the rest of the chapter.[89] The Daniel passage, dated *ca.* 165 B.C., portrays a resurrection of some of the righteous and some of the wicked.

I Enoch 6-36,[90] presents a resurrection for all of the righteous and some of the wicked; the risen righteous eat of the "fragrant tree,"[91] and thereby "live a long life" as did the patriarchs,[92] on the earth, which is

[141]

cleansed from all oppression, unrighteousness, sin, and godlessness,[93] and all the children of men become righteous and worship God.[94] By this writer the resurrection life is portrayed in realistic terms of sense experience. Those wicked only are raised who have not been punished in this life.[95]

The resurrection according to I Enoch 87-90 is for all the righteous and none of the wicked.[96] The Testament of Benjamin teaches a general resurrection:[97]

Then shall ye see Enoch, Noah, and Shem, and Abraham, and Isaac, and Jacob, rising on the right hand in gladness. Then shall we also rise, each one over our tribe, worshiping the King of heaven. . . . Then also all men shall rise, some unto glory and some unto shame. And the Lord shall judge Israel first, for their unrighteousness . . . And then shall he judge all the gentiles.[98]

In I Enoch 91-104,[99] "the righteous shall arise from their sleep,"[100] as imperishable spirits,[101] to whom the portals of heaven are opened,[102] and they "have great joy as the angels of heaven,"[103] being "companions of the hosts of heaven."[104] On the other hand, in I Enoch 37-71,[105] the risen righteous are angelic in nature,[106] and have "garments of glory,"[107] i. e., bodies.

And in those days shall the earth also give back that which has been entrusted to it,

And Sheol also shall give back that which it has received,

And hell shall give back that which it owes,

For in those days the Elect One shall arise,
And he shall choose the righteous and holy from among them:
For the day has drawn nigh that they should be saved.
And the Elect One shall in those days sit on my throne,
And his mouth shall pour forth all the secrets of wisdom and counsel:
For the Lord of Spirits hath given (them) to him and hath glorified him.
And in those days shall the mountains leap like rams,
And the hills also shall skip like lambs satisfied with milk,
And the faces of (all) the angels in heaven shall be lighted up with joy
And the earth shall rejoice,
And the righteous shall dwell upon it,
And the elect shall walk thereon.[108]

And the Lord of Spirits will abide over them,
And with that Son of Man shall they eat
And lie down and rise up for ever and ever.
And the righteous and elect shall have risen from the earth,
And ceased to be of downcast countenance.
And they shall have been clothed with garments of glory,
And these shall be the garments of life from the Lord of Spirits:
And your garments shall not grow old,
Nor your glory pass away before the Lord of Spirits.[109]

The literature of the first century A.D. exhibits variety of opinion in Palestinian Judaism on the subject of the resurrection, which proves that the belief was by no means standardized or dogmatized. The Assumption of Moses is not explicit, but seems to maintain the resurrection of the righteous in the spirit only.[110] Such had been the doctrine of Jubilees,[111] already in the first century B.C. The resurrection of the righteous in a spiritual body is the doctrine of II Enoch,[112] and of Josephus.[113] The resurrection in the body of all mankind is, however, the doctrine of II Baruch and IV Ezra.

Then all who have fallen asleep in hope of him shall rise again. And it shall come to pass at that time that the treasuries will be opened in which is preserved the number of the souls of the righteous, and they shall come forth, and a multitude of souls shall be seen together in one assemblage of one thought, and the first shall rejoice and the last shall not be grieved. For they know that the time has come of which it is said, that it is the consummation of the times. But the souls of the wicked, when they behold all these things, shall then waste away the more. For they shall know that their torment has come and their perdition has arrived.[114]

In what shape will those live who live in thy day?
Or how will the splendor of those who (are) after that time continue?[115]

For the earth shall then assuredly restore the dead,
(Which it now receives in order to preserve them.)
It shall make no change in their form,

[144]

But as it has received, so shall it restore them,
And as I delivered them unto it, so also shall it raise
them.[116]

The earth shall restore those that sleep in her, and the
dust those that are at rest therein, (and the chambers shall
restore those that were committed unto them.)[117]

The resurrection was realistically conceived. It was
a resurrection of the buried body, taking place upon
the earth. The blessings of the righteous and the pun-
ishments of the wicked were also realistically conceived.
Jewish thought did not dematerialize the spiritual
existence after death.

Jesus' teaching regarding immortality was discussed
in Chapter III as a feature of his teaching on the value
of personality. The passage which preserves this teaching is not connected with the general eschatological
teaching in the synoptic gospels.[118] Jesus does not argue
for immortality on the eschatological basis of the neces-
sity of the resurrection in order to the judgment, but
rather he grounds the belief in the goodness of God.
Jesus did not speculate about the nature of the resurrection body or portray the immortal life in any such
realistic or fantastic imagery as is found in some of the
apocalyptists. Jesus is content merely to proclaim the
assurance of a blessed future life for the righteous. To
him the resurrection life is an ethical and logical neces-

sity in view of God's purpose to bring to pass a society of the righteous, i. e., of the sons of God.

In Jewish eschatology the oldest idea, and the basal idea, is that of a day of judgment, with which are regularly associated two further ideas standard in Jewish apocalyptic, viz., eternal punishment for the wicked and eternal life for the righteous. The idea of a day of judgment developed from the Old Testament conception of the Day of Yahweh. Down to the eighth century, B.C., a popular conception of the Day of Yahweh was that of the day when Yahweh would overthrow the nation's enemies and inaugurate an unbroken era of national prosperity for Israel. With Amos the idea became that of a day of doom directed against Israel, a day of Yahweh's vindication, not of the nation but of his own righteous purposes.[119] Isaiah similarly declared that the day was directed not only against Israel but against Judah as well.[120] The judgment of the nations was, of course, included in the judgment against the chosen people, but the conception of a world judgment is later than Isaiah. Zephaniah portrayed the Day of Yahweh as a day of wrath upon the whole world,[121] from which a righteous remnant of Israel would survive.[122] With the exilic prophets, beginning with Jeremiah,[123] the conception of collective punishment for national guilt yielded to that of individual retribution in the judgment. Ezekiel portrays a judgment in which the heathen are destroyed and a purged Israel emerges.[124] Joel approximates the idea of a final judgment in his conception of Yahweh's judgment of the nations in the valley of Jehoshaphat.[125] The idea of a universal final world judgment comes fully into view in Daniel 7. In the apocalyptical literature the judgment is variously viewed as taking place either at the advent of the kingdom or at its close. Judgment on the living and on certain classes of the dead at the advent of the kingdom is the view of I Enoch 6-36,[126] and 83-90.[127] Judgment on all rational beings at the beginning of the kingdom is the view of I Enoch 37-71.[128] The judgment on all rational beings as coming at the close of the kingdom is the view of Jubilees,[129] I Enoch 91-104,[130] and Psalms of Solomon 17;[131] also of II Enoch,[132] and IV Ezra.[133]

Throughout all this literature the central thought is that history is leading up to a great transition. This is the Jewish philosophy of history. Again the basis is ethical. Jewish ethical impulse felt keenly the consciousness of sin as well as the urge to righteousness and demanded that righteousness prevail in man and in the world. The logical issue of such an ethical demand is that men will be held to accountability for their deeds. This is the ethical basis of the idea of the day of judgment. The judgment will sift out and conserve whatever is of ethical value in the present age and with this the new age will be integrated. Apocalyptical literature expresses advanced faith, idealism, and cosmic speculation. It arose to satisfy ethical demands.

The day of judgment was the main theme in the preaching of John the Baptist. He regarded it as imminent.[134] The ethical test alone would be decisive at the judgment.[135] John, therefore, used this idea as a powerful incentive to right ethical conduct.[136]

The synoptic gospels present the idea of the judgment as a part of the eschatology of Jesus. Jesus explicitly disclaims the possibility of any knowledge concerning the day or the hour of the judgment.[137] Perhaps he considered it to be imminent, as did John the Baptist, to occur before the passing of the existing generation.[138] In any case it would come suddenly and unexpectedly.[139] Jesus' idea of the judgment was, like other aspects of his world-view, ethically based. It was characteristic of Jesus to emphasize the inward side of truth in his ethical teaching. In the Sermon on the Mount he emphasizes inward motives and declares that "thy Father, who seeth in secret, shall recompense thee."[140] Consistent with this teaching is his parable concerning the judgment of the Son of Man.[141] The righteous are there depicted as not knowing what they had done to merit the kingdom.[142] This parable is significant as showing the ethical basis of the judgment, which is according to deeds.[143] Any view of the judgment would be impossible without the assumption of the punishment of the wicked. This appears as a conventional feature in Jesus' view and is likewise ethically based, as seen in the parable of the talents.[144] This is a parable of judgment. The men were left on their own responsibility and they were held to account in the day of reckoning. "Fear him who is able to destroy both soul and body in Gehenna."[145] "The men of Nineveh shall stand up in the judgment with this generation, and shall condemn it," because they accepted the prophetic preaching and repented.[146] "The Queen of the South shall rise up in the judgment with this generation, and shall condemn it," because she recognized the value of wisdom teaching.[147] The rejection of such truth brings condemnation in the judgment. So does the refusal to forgive.[148] Condemnation as well as approval is on the basis of deeds.[149] In the woes upon the unbelieving cities Jesus declared that it would be "more tolerable in the day of judgment" for Tyre and Sidon, or for Sodom, than for them.[150] Apparently Jesus thus purposely left the question of the amount and duration of punishment indefinite. It is more tolerable for some than for others. One would, therefore, suspect the assignment of "eternal punishment" in "eternal fire,"[151] as representing the standardized view of the evangelist more than it does Jesus' view.[152] Whether due to the evangelist or to Jesus, it is typical Oriental exaggeration.[153] Jesus is not primarily concerned with the punishment of the wicked. We may be sure that whatever view he held of the matter would not be inconsistent with his principle of love toward one's enemies, which applies to God as well as man, for Jesus exhorts his hearers to make God's attitude their own.[154]

What Jesus is primarily concerned with is the reward of the righteous. The ethical values which Jesus proclaimed in his teaching have ultimate survival value. That is what the judgment signifies. It signifies, however, not alone the survival of certain ethical values, but still more *the arrival of the highest of all ethical values, eternal life in the kingdom of God*. It is in the direction of this that all of Jesus' thought is oriented. Not the judgment, but *beyond the judgment* is the determining consideration in the philosophy of Jesus.

Chapter VII

THE KINGDOM OF GOD

In Chapter IV we discussed the place of the promises in the popular Jewish philosophy of history. The anticipation was for a future era of national blessedness. In popular thought this era was to be inaugurated by the Day of Yahweh, when Israel's enemies would be destroyed and endless material prosperity would commence. This popular view was non-moral. The prophetic idea of the kingdom, however, embraces two ethical considerations: the nation is to be regenerated in the new age and in the regenerated community the divine will is to be fulfilled. Such is the idea of Isaiah,[1] and Zephaniah.[2] The prevailing note, however, among the pre-exilic prophets is that of doom on the nation as a nation. In the exilic and post-exilic period the messianic kingdom is foremost in prophetic expectation. The conception of the kingdom was universalistic with Jeremiah,[3] Second Isaiah,[4] Psalms 22, 65, 86, 87,[5] Malachi,[6] and Isaiah 19.[7] A particularistic conception of the kingdom was taught by others, as Ezekiel,[8] some post-exilic fragments in Isaiah,[9] Haggai,[10] Zechariah,[11] Joel,[12] and Daniel.[13]

The particularistic conception dominates the apocryphal and apocalyptical writings. In I Enoch 6-36 the kingdom is conceived as one which will exist on the present earth and as an everlasting state of material prosperity.[14] Despite the abundant sensuous imagery of this writer, there is a fine ethical note:

> And in those days I will open the store chambers of blessing which are in the heaven, so as to send them down upon the earth over the work and labor of the children of men. And truth and peace shall be associated together throughout all the days of the world and throughout all the generations of men.[15]

A similar conception is in II Maccabees.[16] I Enoch 83-90 adds to this picture the conception of the New Jerusalem as the center of this kingdom.[17] The idea of a messianic kingdom of eternal duration on the present earth is abandoned by the writers of the first century B.C., because of the dualistic element in their thinking which set the things of earth and the things of heaven in sharp antithesis. I Enoch 91-104 regards the messianic kingdom as of temporary duration, concluding with the judgment.[18] A new heaven is created, to share in which the righteous rise from the dead.[19] The Psalms of Solomon regard the messianic kingdom as temporary and do not depict the righteous as rising to share in it;[20]

the righteous rise to life eternal.[21] Jubilees expects a gradual advent of the kingdom which ends at the day of judgment.[22] The Assumption of Moses likewise regards the kingdom as temporary, at the close of which Israel is to be exalted to heaven.[23] In II Enoch and II Baruch the length of the kingdom is a millennium, ending with the judgment.[24] IV Ezra makes the length of the kingdom 400 years.[25] In all of these writers the conception of the kingdom is realistic, though not without an ethical element, for the blessedness is for the righteous, and sin and evil have no place in the kingdom. In all cases the inauguration of the kingdom is catastrophic, by divine fiat. The conception in all its phases is rather mechanical.

The writer of I Enoch 37-71 presents a different conception from the foregoing. He regards the kingdom as a spiritual kingdom enduring eternally in a *new* heaven and a *new* earth, in which the righteous will be like angels and will be companions of the hosts of heaven.[26]

Jewish thought always regarded the sovereignty of God under the two aspects of present and future. Both appear in the Old Testament. God was always regarded as the present sovereign in a special sense of his chosen people, and to some extent of the heathen. The sin and disobedience of Israel, however, made God's rule over the nation only a germ of what it would be when all Israel as well as all the nations rendered him homage.

Thus the most characteristic conception of the kingdom came to be the future conception. The eschatological kingdom was predominant in the thought of later Judaism, as has appeared in the preceding survey.

From one point of view the Jewish idea of the kingdom of God was abstract—the sovereignty, or rule, or kingship of God.[27] This is the primary meaning of *Basileia tou theou*. From another point of view the idea was concrete, meaning the divine community, or social order, in which the will of God would be perfectly done, i. e., the rule of God as realized in the lives of the righteous.

In view of this background we must inquire in how far Jesus' doctrine of the kingdom was eschatological. E. F. Scott rightly says:

His conception of the kingdom cannot be wholly interpreted by means of the apocalyptic tradition. It is impregnated with new religious ideas, and needs to be examined in the light of his own teaching.[28]

The question whether Jesus regarded the kingdom as present or future involves a false alternative. Jesus regarded it as *both* present *and* future.[29] In the thinking of Jesus the kingdom is God's kingdom, that is, the stress falls upon the word God rather than upon the word kingdom. God's kingdom is God's manner of rule. Jesus is principally concerned to teach what kind of king God is and is going to be. As has been pointed out, Jesus' theory of reality is: God is present and at work in his world. God is the Eternal. He rules now and he will rule in the future.

Jesus regarded the various factors in his world-view from the standpoint of inwardness. In his attitude toward the law, for example, he regards the supremely important thing to be the inward motive which lies behind the external commandments;[30] for example, "Give for alms those things which are within,"[31] which Goodspeed so well renders: "Give thine inmost self for charity." Similarly in his estimate of man he directed his teaching to the inner nature, to the soul of man, and it is the spiritual worth of man as a self which he makes central. We would, therefore, fully expect Jesus to transfer this technique to apocalyptic and to regard this also from the inward side. It is from this point of view that he does consider the kingdom of God. The passage which explicitly states this is:

And being asked by the Pharisees, when the kingdom of God cometh, he answered them and said, The kingdom of God cometh not with observation; neither shall they say, Lo, here! or, There! for lo, the kingdom of God is within you.[32]

This statement means that the kingdom of God is an existing reality awaiting discovery by those who take the right attitude toward it. Jesus made this point abundantly clear in parables illustrative of the kingdom, e. g., the parables of the leaven, the mustard seed, and the seed growing secretly. It is noteworthy that these parables are, in the synoptic records, given in passages entirely disconnected with the eschatological discourses, which is evidence that the synoptists fully understood Jesus to have proclaimed the doctrine of the kingdom in other than eschatological terms. The parable of the leaven directs attention to a present reality which, though hidden, and though small, is nevertheless a force at work.[33] When all is leavened it is in quality just like the small lump with which the housewife began. There is an inner side to the process, a mysterious working. Similarly with the planted seed, be it wheat or mustard seed, you know that in the end you will have a harvest of what you sow, wheat or mustard. As illustrative of the kingdom of God, the point of emphasis is not the smallness of the beginning, and certainly not gradual development, but rather that its essential nature is a present reality. You know what it is going to be like in the eschatological climax, because you may know what it is like in the present, and Jesus' dominant concern is to teach what it *is* like. Jesus views life *sub specie aeternitatis*. His ethical ideal is set forth as that kind of life which characterizes those who now are sons of God and which will be the kind of life all live in the fully consummated kingdom of God.[34] The kingdom of God is like a treasure hidden in a field,[35] or like a very valuable pearl which awaits discovery by the persistent seeker.[36] The kingdom type of life is to be found in children,[37] among the poor in spirit,[38] in the discerning scribe,[39] among repentant sinners,[40] even among those of alien race.[41] Boyd Scott well says:

The kingdom must be regarded as a contemporary "presence" of an objective kind. It was there in such form that people who listened to him could and did enter into it. . . . It implies a conviction on the part of Jesus of what is called the objectivity of spiritual values.[42]

The gospels state as the central theme of Jesus' preaching: "The kingdom of God is at hand; repent ye."[43] Jesus' reply to the messengers from John the Baptist enumerates works which evidence the existing reality of the kingdom.[44] Further, the casting out of demons was evidence that "the kingdom of God is come upon you."[45] "Seek ye first his kingdom,"[46] implies that it is something present. So do the sayings: "I beheld Satan fallen as lightning from heaven,"[47] and "Many prophets and righteous men desired to see the things which ye see, and saw them not; and to hear the things which ye hear, and heard them not."[48]

In concluding a discussion of the four parables of the mustard seed, leaven, seed growing secretly, and the sower, B. W. Bacon emphasizes the uniqueness of Jesus' conception of the kingdom:

They show with wonderful clarity Jesus' conception of how God and man coöperate in bringing his kingdom to pass. At that time the idea was new. It differs strikingly from anything you can find in prophecy or apocalypse. It differs profoundly from the message of John.[49] Indeed it is quite unparalleled save for those deeper insights of Paul and the Second Source . . . those utterances about a kingdom "within you" and "among you," a kingdom which is not a messianic banquet of eating and drinking, but "righteousness and peace and joy in the Holy Ghost." Jesus' doctrine of the kingdom was new, distinctive, different. But it was not obscure. It was not hidden. It did not even contradict the old. It only glorified and transfigured it with the touch of one who could see God at work.[50]

Jesus did not speculate concerning the eschatological details of the kingdom. To do so would have been inconsistent with his own faith. The same faith which the patient farmer displays toward the future harvest for which he hopes and labors and waits is the faith one may have toward the eschatological kingdom of God. The great Old Testament prophets were not primarily concerned with detailed predictions about future events. The failure of such forecasts as they did make did not deter them from their work. Their own intense faith led them to make confident assertions concerning the future triumph of righteousness.

In how far Jesus interpreted the apocalyptical teachings of the prophets literally is very difficult to say.

There is no doubt, however, that he genuinely accepted them. In so far as Jesus employed apocalyptical imagery it was to make plain to his hearers in terms they would fully understand his own assurance of the reality of the ultimate triumph of righteousness for which they and he alike hoped. Jesus could not have neglected eschatology and had a complete and consistent world-view. The perspective of the Jewish mind was short. The horizons of time, as of space, were not far stretching. It was easy for them to think that God was ready at any time to intervene. His intervention was regarded as imminent. Consequently Jewish apocalyptical writers indulged in many fantastic speculations regarding the time and manner of the coming of the kingdom. Jesus brushed all that aside with the self-evident truth: "Of that day and hour knoweth no one, not even the angels of heaven, neither the Son, but the Father only."[51] That does not mean, however, that Jesus did not regard the end as imminent. Apparently he did so regard it.

"There are some here of them that stand by, who shall in no wise taste of death, till they see the kingdom of God come with power,"[52] i. e., in its complete development and full strength. This and other passages clearly reflect the idea of the future kingdom. "Thy kingdom come."[53] "Many shall come from the east and west, and shall sit down with Abraham and Isaac

[159]

and Jacob in the kingdom of heaven."[54] "I shall no more drink of the fruit of the vine until that day when I drink it new in the kingdom of God."[55]

Some interpreters stress the idea of gradual development of the kingdom, basing such interpretation on the parables of the leaven and of the growing seed. These parables are, on this basis, usually understood to be in contradiction to the idea of the eschatological, sudden, and miraculous coming of the kingdom. Such modernizing interpretation is to be rejected as foreign to the world-view of Jesus. The developmental or evolutionary thought-form was wholly unknown to Jesus and his contemporaries. It was open to them to observe, of course, the growth of vegetation within a given season, but they never thought of even that as taking place by a process apart from God. There was to them always something miraculous about the harvest, which suddenly and all at once appears. Certainly Jesus worked for and could observe in some measure the extension of his own ideals in an enlarging group of disciples. But what he anticipated was that there would be in the immediate future a sudden and perfect realization of the kingdom, which was to come about through direct divine intervention. The futurity of the kingdom is more pronounced in Jesus' teaching in the latter part of his ministry. Doubtless this was in view of his own rejection by the people, which led him to stress the fact that only the direct intervention of God could achieve the consummation of the kingdom.

A significant aspect of Jesus' doctrine is the identifying of the "kingdom" with "life." This is clear in the Markan passage, "It is good for thee to enter into the kingdom of God with one eye," etc.,[56] which in Matthew reads: "It is good for thee to enter into life with one eye," etc.[57] Even Mark in the same context, presenting a teaching with the same purport, says, "It is good for thee to enter into life maimed," etc.[58] "Narrow is the gate and straitened the way that leadeth unto life."[59] The kingdom as well as life is something which one may *enter into*,[60] and likewise is something which one may inherit, or *receive*. This is clear from the story of the rich young man. "What shall I do that I may inherit eternal life?"[61] "How hardly shall they that have riches enter into the kingdom of God!"[62] Jesus remarked that those who followed him would receive "in the world to come eternal life."[63] The discourse concerning the judgment of the Son of Man promises that the righteous shall "inherit the kingdom."[64]

Jewish eschatology and the eschatology of Jesus are both alike oriented toward the achievement of the ideal humanity in an ideal social order, the kingdom of God. As Montefiore puts it,

The essential feature of the ordinary conception of the messiah was that of a righteous king ruling over a righteous people; the messianic era was indeed one of prosperity, but far more was it one of peace and goodness and the knowledge of God.[65]

The essential idea of the kingdom of God was that in it there would be realized the highest moral and religious ideal. Faith, repentance, and righteousness are the foundations upon which it rests and the conditions of entrance into it. Jesus considers that God's immediate purpose is the establishment of this ideal order.

Chapter VIII

THE REMNANT

In PRECEDING chapters the integration of Jesus' world-view with apocalyptic has been affirmed. It is now in order to correlate the views which have been expressed, so as to show what, if any, original emphasis Jesus made.

The term apocalyptic is technically used in three senses: it designates a literary type, it designates a body of literature of that type, and it designates the set of doctrinal ideas presented in such literature. Otherwise stated, apocalyptic, in this third sense, is a world-view. One aspect of such world-view, as we have pointed out, is the doctrine of the issues of the future, i. e., eschatology. The terms apocalyptic and eschatology are too frequently confused. They are not exact synonyms. Apocalyptic is the more inclusive term. Eschatology is only one aspect of apocalyptic.

Apocalyptic embraces a doctrine of the past (a philosophy of history), and a doctrine of the present (a social philosophy), as well as a doctrine of the future (eschatology). The verb *apokalypto,* from which the words apocalypse and apocalyptic are derived, means "to reveal." This meaning furnishes a clue for the interpretation of apocalyptic. What does the past reveal? What does the present reveal? What will the future reveal?

As a doctrine of history, apocalyptic holds that the past reveals that at crises God has catastrophically intervened to remove evil and re-establish righteousness. In the beginning of creation, God by a mighty act of irruption destroyed the primeval chaos and established a cosmos, according to ancient Babylonian myth which was assimilated to Jewish thought, as has been pointed out.[1] No allusion to this myth is credited to Jesus, though in a parable he does speak of "the kingdom prepared from the foundation of the world,"[2] implying thereby that an eternal purpose has been in the world from the time of the creation.

The favorite historical illustration of apocalyptists was the flood, which catastrophe marked God's intervention to eradicate evil.[3] Jesus definitely made use of this theory: "As it came to pass in the days of Noah," etc.[4] Jesus also used another example: "Likewise even as it came to pass in the days of Lot," etc.[5] The destruction of Sodom and the cities of the plain was another catastrophe which apocalyptic ascribed to God's incursion into history to eradicate evil.[6] Disasters in the natural world, such as the flood, volcanic eruption (which presumably is what destroyed Sodom), "earthquakes, and in divers places famines and pestilences,"[7] such a notable plague as that of the locusts portrayed in Joel, lent themselves to apocalyptic interpretation as cases of God's cataclysmic intrusion into history to end evil. Not only natural disasters were so viewed; the social disaster of wars was similarly regarded. The great political and social disaster of the exile was likewise so interpreted by Second Isaiah, who, writing about that tragedy, said: "This is as the waters of Noah unto me."[8]

Now just what was it that "came to pass in the days of Noah?" Not only did that catastrophe destroy the sinful race of men, but a righteous remnant survived:

And Yahweh said unto Noah, Come thou and all thy house into the ark; for thee have I seen righteous before me in this generation.[9]

This remnant God made the unit for the re-establishing of the world; Noah became the new progenitor of mankind. There was a like inward side to the disaster which "came to pass in the days of Lot." The account in Gen. 18:22-33 of Abraham's intercession with God on behalf of the righteous few of Sodom is one of the very finest Old Testament passages setting forth the doctrine of the righteous, or holy, remnant.

The idea of a remnant is that of a small nucleus of spiritually minded and morally upright people around whom God can order the new day. Therefore this remnant will survive the devastation of the "Day of Yahweh." The eighth-century prophet Amos first expressed the idea:

Hate the evil, and love the good, and establish justice in the gate: it may be that Yahweh, the God of hosts, will be gracious unto the remnant of Joseph.[10]

The idea apparently held a central place in the thinking of Isaiah, so much so that he named one of his sons Shear-jashub, "A remnant shall return."[11] The idea is developed in various passages in the book of Isaiah which scholars generally regard as later insertions;[12] one passage, regarded by some as genuine, presents the idea in a picturesque way:

Yet there shall be left therein gleanings, as the shaking of an olive-tree, two or three berries in the top of the uppermost bough, four or five in the outmost branches of a fruitful tree, saith Yahweh, the God of Israel.[13]

Isa. 28:16 expresses this idea of a remnant under wholly different imagery; Yahweh lays in Zion a precious cornerstone of sure foundation. Zephaniah stated the idea as follows:

In that day shalt thou not be put to shame for all thy doings, wherein thou hast transgressed against me; for then I will take away out of the midst of thee thy proudly exulting ones, and thou shalt no more be haughty in my holy

[166]

mountain. But I will leave in the midst of thee an afflicted and poor people, and they shall take refuge in the name of Yahweh. The remnant of Israel shall not do iniquity, nor speak lies; neither shall a deceitful tongue be found in their mouth; for they shall feed and lie down, and none shall make them afraid.[14]

Ezekiel expressed the idea of the remnant as follows:

Thus saith the Lord Yahweh: I will also take of the lofty top of the cedar, and will set it; I will crop off from the topmost of its young twigs a tender one, and I will plant it upon a high and lofty mountain: in the mountain of the height of Israel will I plant it; and it shall bring forth boughs, and bear fruit, and be a goodly cedar: and under it shall dwell all birds of every wing; in the shade of the branches thereof shall they dwell.[15]

Of course, this doctrine of the remnant was applied to the interpretation of the meaning of the exile itself.

What is to happen in the future must be judged by what has happened in the past, especially if it be true that "That which hath been is that which shall be; and that which hath been done is that which shall be done; and there is no new thing under the sun."[16] Therefore apocalyptic said: "As it came to pass in the days of Noah, even so shall it be also in the days of the Son of man."[17] In applying the apocalyptic thought-pattern to the issues of the future, the conventional eschatology laid stress upon "the last evils," which precipitate the Parousia and are destroyed at the judgment. But what righteous remnant will then be available for God's use as a nucleus on which to establish his kingdom of righteousness? "When the Son of Man cometh, shall he find faith on the earth?"[18] is the way Jesus put this question. This brings us to the apocalyptic view of the present age.

The apocalyptic doctrine of the past is that certain great catastrophes have marked God's incursion into history to destroy evil and re-establish the earth in righteousness, building upon a surviving remnant as a nucleus. The doctrine of eschatology is that the future will witness, at the Parousia, God's catastrophic irruption into history again to remove evil and establish his kingdom of righteousness. What was the apocalyptic doctrine of the present, its social philosophy, if such expression may be allowed? In the conventional view, the present is a time of rampant evil, which God ought to intervene to stop.

Jesus held the view that evil was rampant in his age. He characterized his age as a "faithless and perverse, an evil and adulterous generation."[19] He criticised blameworthy social attitudes prevalent in his day, as reflected in the parables of the unjust steward,[20] and the unjust judge;[21] in the attitudes which prompt men to go to law;[22] in the tyrannous attitude of rulers;[23] and in the attitude of "men of violence" toward the kingdom of God.[24] God's elect cry out day and night for justice.[25] There were "lovers of money, the mammon of unrighteousness."[26] The sense of values was perverted: "That which is exalted among men is an abomination in the sight of God."[27] The Beatitudes disclose not only that there were people who suffered, but that there were those who deliberately caused such suffering, those who reproached, and persecuted, and spoke all manner of evil falsely.[28] Social misery stirred Jesus' compassion: "He saw a great multitude, and he had compassion on them, because they were as sheep not having a shepherd."[29]

Such castigation of the evil age was not the end of the matter with Jesus. Therein he differed from John the Baptist, who saw mainly the evil of the age, in view of which he held that God's immediate purpose was judgment. Jesus was positive rather than negative in his outlook. In keeping with this and with his characteristic principle of inwardness, Jesus stressed the inward side of apocalyptical thought. Now the inward side of apocalyptic is the doctrine of the remnant, and it is in his attitude at this point that Jesus shows genuine originality. If Jesus' originality is to be found in the depth of his re-thinking of Jewish doctrines, then surely this is to be observed in his re-thinking of apocalyptic. Here, as also with regard to the law, Jesus came "not to destroy but to fulfill." This phase of his world-view cannot be calculated mechanically by merely calling attention to standard Jewish apocalyptical doctrine. Jesus brought forth things new.

When Jesus contemplated what to him was the present, what was its inward aspect? It was that a holy remnant was and ought to be in the making, which would be available for God's use at the Parousia as a nucleus with which to integrate his kingdom. Hence Jesus summoned men to discipleship. The disciples were to constitute such a holy remnant. T. W. Manson expresses the view:

The kingdom of God is manifested on earth and in the present in the existence of human subjects who own God as their King, who look to him for protection, guidance, and a rule of life, who offer to him their absolute loyalty, complete trust, and willing obedience. That is the ideal. Wherever it is to any extent realized, there we have the Remnant.[30]

Theirs was to be the blessing, not of escaping the terrors of the judgment merely to enter into bliss, but of being available then for God to make the core of his kingdom. "Fear not, little flock; for it is your Father's good pleasure to give you the kingdom."[31] "Little flock" implies the remnant idea. The parable of the patient farmer contains the philosophy of discipleship.[32] The farmer does his part by preparing the soil and planting the seed; he leaves the results with God, for he knows that God is active. So Jesus prepared a holy remnant of disciples, and knowing that God is active, the results were left with him. That is why Jesus declined to speculate concerning the time of the Parousia: "Of that day or that hour knoweth no one."[33] But further, the sower knows that in the harvest what is reaped will be exactly like what is planted, wheat or barley, and what is planted is literally a remnant, seed saved from the previous harvest. The same doctrine is in the parable of the leaven: "The kingdom of heaven is like unto leaven," which also is literally a remnant saved from the previous baking, and when the batch of dough is "all leavened," it will be like the remnant which the housewife "took and hid in three measures of meal."[34] So it was to be with the eschatological kingdom of God; it would be integrated with the surviving remnant as a nucleus, and would be like the remnant. Hence the remnant of disciples now in the making is a projection of the kingdom into the present. This is the implication of the remark attributed to Jesus in Luke's narrative of the return of the seventy disciples from their missionary deputation with the report that "even the demons are subject unto us in thy name;"[35] Jesus said, "In this rejoice not, that the spirits are subject unto you; but rejoice that your names are written in heaven."[36] Names written in heaven made them heirs of the kingdom and hence the nucleus of the kingdom

[171]

already on earth, i. e., the remnant.[37] This is what is meant by interpreters who speak of the present, or the proleptic, kingdom, or realized eschatology. The present remnant is the inward aspect of society.

Jesus must not be modernized by reading present-day attitudes back into his age. This is precisely the fallacy, though committed in the name of historical interpretation, of those who brand the apocalyptic outlook as a defeatist attitude, wherein man throws up his hands in despair because evil is so potent, and calls upon God to put an end to it. Quite the contrary was the case with Jesus. Appreciation of the inward side of this apocalyptical attitude stimulated him to form a company of disciples, not as an esoteric group, but as a missionary group. Jesus sent his disciples out on deputation work. They were sent as lambs (a minority, or remnant, indeed) in the midst of wolves (an evil society);[38] the laborers were few (a remnant), though the harvest was plenteous.[39]

In commissioning his disciples, Jesus anticipated that, where they preached, some who heard their message would be sympathetically responsive, and when the disciples quit a town, there would be a remnant left behind.[40] "Narrow is the gate, and straitened the way, that leadeth unto life, and few are they that find it."[41] "Many are called, but few chosen,"[42] is the concluding

[172]

verse of the parable of the slighted invitation, which parable implies choice and free will on the part of those who rejected the invitation.[43] The idea of a remnant is implicit in Jesus' giving of thanks that God had revealed his truths not to the learned but to children.[44]

The kind of life which Jesus set forth in his ethical teaching and to which his hearers were summoned to be disciples, is "eternal" life, i. e., the kind of life all will live in the fully consummated kingdom of God.[45] The bed-rock ethical principle on which the entire structure of Jesus' ethical teaching rests is the Golden Rule. In his formulation of the Golden Rule Jesus was genuinely and uniquely original, and this originality consists in the fact that Jesus stated it positively rather than negatively. Jewish wisdom teaching antecedent to Jesus contains the Golden Rule, but always in the negative form. The earliest occurrence and the briefest form in which it has ever been stated (exactly four words in the Greek) is in Tobit:

What you hate, to no one do.[46]

The Letter of Aristeas gives it:

What is the teaching of wisdom? As you wish that no evil should befall you, but to be a partaker of all good things, so you should act on the same principle towards your subjects and offenders, and you should mildly admonish the noble and good.[47]

[173]

Rabbi Hillel put it:

Whatsoever thou wouldest that men should not do unto thee, do not do that to them.[48]

Philo, the Jewish philosopher of Alexandria, expressed it:

What you hate to endure, do not yourself do.[49]

The negative form of the Golden Rule restrains man from contributing in any way to the propagation of evil. The positive form enjoins man to be aggressive in propagating the good; it is, therefore, creative. By the positive formulation of the Golden Rule Jesus aimed to sublimate the most basic drive in human nature, the impulse to retaliate. As a person treats others, he may expect to be treated. Man instinctively returns evil for evil, and is likely to return good for good; only the pervert returns evil for good, and only the saint returns good for evil. This principle came to expression in the Old Testament.

Say not, I will do so to him as he hath done to me;
I will render to the man according to his work.[50]

Say not thou, I will recompense evil.[51]

Say ye of the righteous, that it shall be well with him; for they shall eat of the fruit of their doings.

Woe unto the wicked! it shall be ill with him; for what his hands have done shall be done unto him.[52]

If a man cause a blemish in his neighbor, as he hath done, so shall it be done to him.[53]

For the day of Yahweh is near upon all the nations; as thou hast done, it shall be done unto thee; thy dealing shall return upon thine own head.[54]

Jesus, of course, did not have to have the Scriptures teach him this, for it is human nature in the raw. He knew that "all they that take the sword shall perish with the sword."[55] He definitely came to grips with this retaliation principle in the Sermon on the Mount. "Ye have heard that it was said, An eye for an eye, and a tooth for a tooth; but I say unto you, Resist not him that is evil." His disciples were not, however, to be passively non-resistant; they were to be aggressive in another way: "Whosoever smiteth thee on thy right cheek, turn to him the other also. And if any man would go to law with thee, and take away thy coat, let him have thy cloak also. And whosoever shall compel thee to go one mile, go with him two."[56]

The setting in which the Golden Rule is placed in the gospels is very significant as revealing Jesus' social philosophy. In Matthew it climaxes the passage in which Jesus discusses the ideal social attitude (Matt. 7:1-12). The universe is so constituted that it responds

[175]

to the person who energetically takes the initiative: "Every one that asketh receiveth; and he that seeketh findeth; and to him that knocketh it shall be opened."[57] This is true also in social relations: "With what measure ye mete, it shall be measured unto you." Man gets as good as he sends. "With what judgment ye judge, ye shall be judged."[58] Indeed, one is likely to get more than one sends. Just as the aggressive evil-doer provokes a response in the form of retaliatory evil, so the aggressive doer of good provokes a response in generosity: "Give, and it shall be given unto you; good measure, pressed down, shaken together, running over, shall they give into your bosom."[59] This way of treating other people is basic to the creation of an ideal social order. Men of good will are to take the initiative and be aggressive in doing good; such is the injunction of the Golden Rule in its positive form.

"All things whatsoever ye would that men should do unto you," calls upon man to think out, with the aid of his spiritual imagination, the ideal in human relationships. "Do ye even so," means to take such ideal and aggressively provoke others to a response in kind. By this technique the retaliation spirit can be employed to establish good. In view of such considerations, it is manifest that Jesus was not visionary or Utopian in his world-view. Idealistic he certainly was, but his idealism was predicated upon the innate urge of human nature. He could not have been more realistic.

Though this attitude on Jesus' part fitted into the frame-work of apocalyptic, it transcended apocalyptic. Hereby we see how Jesus was creative in his thinking. He sublimated apocalyptic. Whatever may be said for the doctrine of the relativity of ethics does not apply to the Golden Rule. It is absolute. It is not possible to imagine a time, a place, or a situation in which it ever was or ever would be right for any person to treat another as he would not wish to be treated himself, or not to treat another as he would himself wish to be treated. The principle of the Golden Rule has been universally apprehended by the mind of man. One finds it clear across the ancient world, in the sacred books of Confucianism and of Taoism in China; in the Mahabharata of Hinduism and in the literature of Buddhism; in Zoroastrianism; in Judaism; and in Greek philosophy.[60] Of all such statements only two can be termed positive. One is from Taoism:

To those who are good to me, I am good; and to those who are not good to me, I am also good. And thus all get to be good. To those who are sincere with me, I am sincere; and to those who are not sincere with me, I am also sincere. And thus all get to be sincere.[61]

The other is ascribed to Aristotle:

Treat your friends as you would want them to treat you.[62]

Affirmative as these are, they lack the universality of Jesus' statement. Jesus set no limits. The genuine originality of Jesus in the formulation of the Golden Rule is undeniable.

Here, then, in the Golden Rule Jesus enunciated a principle which burst the apocalyptic thought-pattern. That is exactly what happened historically at the end of the first century, A.D. Apocalyptic then passed out of vogue in Christianity. Revelation was the last apocalypse produced. What survived thereafter was not the apocalyptic but the eternal in the world-view of Jesus. What Jesus started emerged in the early Christian community with the precise meaning and emphasis he had intended. The *ecclesia* was the holy remnant; the early Christians deemed themselves to be continuous with the remnant of Israel, i. e., the true Israel within the nation, those who were faithful to the higher calling of Israel, through whom God would work out his purposes.[63] "Even so then at this present time also there is a remnant," wrote St. Paul.[64] The members of the Christian *ecclesia* were most commonly called saints, i. e., "holy ones," in the exact meaning of the Greek (*hagioi*). They were aggressive with the gospel message, their missionary activity occupying the bulk of the book of Acts. Though emphatically eschatological in outlook, they were anything but defeatist. They were God's fellow-workers,[65] and God cannot be defeated. H. E. Fosdick judges the matter soundly:

In so far as the influence of apocalyptic hopes can be clearly discerned, they seem to have positively heightened and clarified moral ideas and ideals. They faced the early Christians with the absolute demands of God's realized sovereignty, confronted them with an imminent kingdom of perfect righteousness, and so called out not small prudential counsels for getting on in this world, but the highest, most unqualified insights as to eternal values.[66]

Jesus employed a language (Aramaic) and a thought-form (apocalyptic) which his own people could understand. Both the language and the thought-form ceased to be. But both served as the vehicle for an ethical principle in the teaching of Jesus which transcended and outlived the apocalyptic thought-pattern of his age, which also could transcend and outlive the thought-pattern of any age, because it is inherently of universal and eternal validity. Its validity is the same in the twentieth century as in the first, and it is not subject to invalidation by changing views concerning the structure of the material universe or by changing social patterns. So long as there are human beings to enter into relationships with one another, the Golden Rule must be basic to any organization of such relationships which looks toward the arrival of the ideal society. Toward the arrival of the ideal society, the kingdom of God, is exactly the direction in which Jesus faced.

Chapter IX

ENDURING VALUES

IN THE preceding chapters the world-view of Jesus has been examined in its details. It must now be considered as a totality. There are specific elements in it which may be judged to be of enduring value. An atomistic examination of it does not, however, disclose all of its value. It must be appraised as a whole, as well as in its constituent elements.

When thus considered as a whole, the question presents itself: Was Jesus in any sense an original thinker? It was pointed out in several instances in the preceding chapters that there are elements in the world-view of Jesus which are identical with the prevailing Jewish world-view of his time. Jesus was not isolated from but rather was genetically connected with the thought life of his time. This likeness of the teaching of Jesus to the contemporary Jewish teaching is stressed by not a few writers.[1] Klausner, for example, states without reservation: "Throughout the gospels there is not one item of ethical teaching which cannot be paralleled either in the Old Testament, the Apocrypha, or in the talmudic and midrashic literature of the period near to the time of Jesus."[2] The question whether and in what respects Jesus was original in his world-view and in his ethical teaching is likewise receiving attention at the present time from writers who stress the originality of Jesus.[3]

No man is simply a product of his environment to be calculated mechanically.

> The new in the history of ideas is never wholly new, nor the old wholly old. . . . Nothing can be wholly new in the sense that it is out of relation to its background and environment, yet nothing wholly old if it has to do with living human beings. The background is never sufficient to explain human persons and happenings, though some historians write as if it were.[4]

Jesus cannot be explained wholly by pointing out what any ordinary first-century Jew would have believed. His world-view is not the echo of the common creed of his time. Because someone else said a thing before Jesus said it, or had ideas similar to his, does not rate down the significance of his saying it. Because we can find the origin of some of his ideas in the current Jewish literature does not argue that in the thinking and teaching of Jesus these ideas were only what they were to other Jews of his day. What happened to these ideas when they were taken up into the mind of Jesus? Surely something creative happened, just as something creative happens to hydrogen and oxygen when they come together and form water. A new thing has emerged, which has a new meaning and value. Jesus was no mere representative of standard scribal Judaism.

"Originality is not measured by the amount of change, but by the depths of re-thinking."[5] The numerous resemblances that various writers point out between the teachings of Jesus and other Jewish, especially rabbinical, teachings would seem to leave Jesus little originality unless the depth and insight with which Jesus re-thought these teachings is appreciated.[6] Jesus was a creative thinker in respect of the new and profound seriousness with which he took old ideas which had been little more than pious formulae, the Fatherhood of God, for example.

The history of religion is brought forward not so much by the appearance of new thoughts as by old thoughts being taken with an entirely new seriousness.[7]

Montefiore emphasizes both the old and the new in Jesus' teaching. In some particulars he considers Jesus' teaching inferior to that of the rabbis, but he does insist repeatedly upon the genuine and epoch-making originality of Jesus. "Through the gospel mists and miracles a character seems to emerge in many respects unlike that of any Old Testament or rabbinic hero, teacher, or saint."[8] Jesus was "a new phenomenon among the Jews, which has scarcely been repeated."[9] Jesus was original in the *sort* of prophet he was, a kind of new Hosea or Isaiah. He was original in his attitude toward the ceremonial law, including the law of the sabbath and its developments. Specific teachings of Jesus which Montefiore regards as highly original are the idea of redemption;[10] the principle of deliberate self-sacrifice;[11] the teaching about clean and unclean things;[12] the teaching about greatness through service and humility;[13] the teaching about divorce;[14] the non-legalistic basis of divine approval in the parable of the laborers in the vineyard;[15] the value which Jesus ascribed to every human soul;[16] Jesus' use of the term Father for God;[17] the Beatitudes taken as a whole.[18] These particular points plus certain general considerations—"the comparatively homogeneous body of doctrine, all attributed to one man, the unity of spirit, the beauty of form, what Jesus does not say as well as what he does, the passion and intensity of the whole"—produce a "total impression of originality."[19]

Goguel likewise finds Jesus original with respect to his idea of God:

Like the Jews of his own time, Jesus believed in a God who is perfect, omnipotent, and omniscient. But—and this is where his originality becomes evident—he places all the emphasis upon the practical consequences . . . of the divine attributes. He does not insist on a theory of omnipotence and omniscience, but he speaks of the God who counts every hair on the heads of his children, without whose permission not a sparrow can fall to the ground. . . . But above all, the unique originality of Jesus consists in his sense of the presence of God, in that conscious and living communion with God in which he lives.[20]

In the preceding chapter on the Remnant, we have stated our own view of just wherein Jesus' unique originality appears in his formulation of the Golden Rule.[21]

In the shaping of his own world-view Jesus found all necessary materials at hand and he worked with them as he found them and made them the vehicle of his fresh insight. What he considered vital he selected and analyzed into its essential principles, laying emphasis upon intrinsic values and inward motives. These principles and values he apprehended in their ultimate relationships. Jesus did not aim to construct a fresh system of knowledge. From the knowledge that was already available he selected that to which his own experience responded as vital and this he infused with a dynamic that made it thenceforth creative, thus providing the life of man with an inner and energizing principle which integrates the total personality.

Many of the elements of the standard first-century world-view are no longer tenable. The ancient cosmology, which was set forth in Chapter II, has been displaced by the modern development of natural science.

The universe is no longer regarded as three-storied in structure, nor is the earth flat. Supernaturalism has yielded to naturalism as a basic mode of thought. The static has given way to the evolutionary in all types of thinking. It was pointed out in Chapter II that Jesus did not expound, expand, or emphasize such ideas about the cosmos. He merely employed them as his contemporaries understood them in order to make intelligible the spiritual aspects of his teaching.

The same criticism applies to the biblical psychology. Although its terms still dominate present-day popular speech, it is no longer the thought-form of technical psychologists. Of that ancient psychology, however, this much does seem to survive modern criticism—that man is a psycho-physical entity, a unitary being, i. e., body-soul, in the ancient terminology.[22] Here again Jesus used the thought-pattern of his age. He understood man's nature as did his contemporaries. He employed this current popular mode of thinking as the vehicle for expressing an insight which is one of the enduring values in his world-view, namely, his estimate of the absolute worth of human personality. This is not only one of the original elements in his world-view,[23] but also one of his permanent contributions to humanity. This estimate of the incalculable value of every human life makes Jesus' ethics fundamentally a social ethics.

In Chapter IV, Jesus' idea of God was considered.

The conception of God as Father was not a new thing in Judaism. It is found in the Old Testament, in the Apocrypha and Pseudepigrapha, and in the later rabbinic literature. G. F. Moore's *Judaism* presents a surprisingly large and impressive collection of such passages.[24] All this to the contrary notwithstanding, Montefiore finds an element of uniqueness in Jesus' use of the term Father for God.

It is apparently a fact that Jesus thought of God as his (and our) Father, and used the term Father for God more habitually and constantly than is the case with any one rabbi of whom we know. And this regular conception of God as Father, in proportion to the intensity and vividness of the feeling which suggested it, was something which may fitly be called original.[25]

The conception of God as Father is one of the enduring values of Jesus' world-view. Indeed we may judge that he selected this idea just because of his perception of its ultimate worth, because it came alive in his own consciousness, expressing all that was most profound and sure in his experience of God.

Jesus' conception of God has a further attribute of enduring value, the *idea of redemption* as expressing the nature of God's activity in the world. What one misses in the passages referred to in Moore's *Judaism* is such a picture of divine Fatherhood as that which Jesus presented in the parable of the lost son.[26] That parable portrays fatherly love as a seeking love, love motivated by a redemptive purpose. In this idea of redemption we have another of the highly original and valuable elements in the world-view of Jesus.[27] This is what in modern terminology would be called a philosophy of the world-process. It is an affirmation of purposiveness in the world-order. More simply put, it is Jesus' idea of God as a Father at work in his world actively redeeming mankind. As an insight which is of enduring value this idea is stressed by Baillie:

It is the crowning excellence of the Christian teaching that this profoundest insight into the implications of the redeeming activity of human love is taken up also into the thought of the redemptive love of God. The divine love is a love that redeems through suffering.[28]

In Chapter IV it was considered that Jesus regarded the world as friendly because he thought of it as the Father's world. A chief reason why he so regarded the universe as friendly was his appreciation of this idea of the redemptive activity of God. He did not stand practically detached from his world-view. It was to him a dynamic conception. He *realized* it in his own ministry. He experienced within himself the impulse to a redemptive ministry and this afforded him an insight into the nature of ultimate reality. Jesus' world-view is characterized by his feeling for reality. He recognized that the real forces in the world are spiritual and he trusted them absolutely, another element of his originality.

For Jesus, God was a clear, living, and present reality. The ethical and religious blend into one in the world-view of Jesus. God to him is good, and is to be found in the good. It is man's moral attitude toward life which makes man aware of the reality of God; the pure in heart see God. This immanent God is to Jesus trustworthy, the one most important force in the universe on which man can count. Jesus is concerned not with what man does but with what man gives God a chance to do through man's right religious attitude. This is basic to his exhortations to repentance and moral endeavor: "Be ye perfect as your Father in heaven is perfect."[29] God is to Jesus the ultimate reality, both present and to come. Jesus did not anticipate that the future would reveal anything essentially different from what he already *realized* as an actuality in his own soul, the very nearness of God and the triumphant power of good. Jesus' conception of God as the ultimate reality, both present and to come, is reflected in his conception of the kingdom of God which, as pointed out in Chapter VII, is a doctrine of the immanence of God.

This emphasis upon immanence in Jesus' conception of the kingdom of God is but one application of Jesus' principle of inwardness, several instances of which principle have been noted in the preceding chapters. It characterized his attitude toward the scriptures,[30] toward the Jewish law,[31] his conception of the realm of nature,[32] his conception of man,[33] of ethical values,[34] of God,[35] and of the future.[36] The principle of inwardness is one of the essential principles of Jesus' world-view. Jesus began where the Ten Commandments left off. The tenth commandment, on covetousness, is the climax of the decalogue and is on the principle of inwardness. It is the most searching of all; the others can be watched as they are broken, but not the tenth. This principle of inwardness is of enduring value. Certainly it is of central significance in the present-day philosophy of values. Values are of two sorts, instrumental and intrinsic, i. e., material and spiritual. Jesus subordinated the material to the intrinsic. The term spiritual is not easy of definition. It is used as a general term to cover all ideal values, intellectual, aesthetic, ethical, social, and religious. All of these values counted with Jesus, certainly, but his specific concern was with ethical and religious values. Praiseworthy moral character is itself one of the most important elements in spirituality. The spiritual values which Jesus stressed are of significance for present-day religious thought. He exalted purity of heart, sincerity, humility, forgiveness, love toward enemies, self-sacrifice and generous service on behalf of others, especially the needy, and above all unworried trust in God. This emphasis upon the spiritual in the world-view of Jesus is very idealistic, and is appreciated as such even by some who disclaim any effort to live by it. All bodily appetites and passions Jesus subordinated strictly to the higher nature of man. Material possessions in his view are not of intrinsic worth. Politics he rated as inferior to righteousness. He stressed love to God and men and faithful devotion to the moral ideal as the very core of spirituality.

The appreciation by Jesus of the relative value of the material and the spiritual is essentially reasonable and of enduring worth. It evidences Jesus' criterion of values. A value is a quality which belongs to any person or thing by virtue of the relationship it has to an end-seeking process. The end-seeking process which Jesus discerns is the present reality and power of those factors which are making for the eschatological, i. e., the ultimate, kingdom of righteousness. In modern terms, Jesus is convinced that ultimately the universe is on the side of the highest values. It is in the light of this ultimate in his thinking that he evaluates persons and things in the present.

Essential in any world-view is a conception of the nature of man's response to the world-process. It is the view of Jesus that in the spiritual environment of man there is this stimulus of the redemptive activity of God, his seeking love. Man's response to this stimulus, in the view of Jesus, consists in faith and co-operation and in a self-sacrificing ministry on behalf of others. The doctrine of deliberate self-sacrifice is another noteworthy item in the world-view of Jesus, both original and of enduring value.

D. C. Macintosh, in his *Reasonableness of Christianity*, has advanced a modern apologetic for the Christian faith. His entire system is based upon the inherent reasonableness of what he designates as "moral optimism." This is one of four possible general attitudes toward reality, life, and destiny.[37] By this term is meant:

A fundamental attitude of confidence in the cosmos, together with a full sense of man's moral responsibility. It expresses and is expressed in the conviction that if only a person's will is right, he need have no fear of anything the universe can do to him; no absolute or final disaster can come to him whose will is steadfastly devoted to the true ideal. . . . It would hold that if man does his best, the Supreme Power on which he is dependent will do whatever else needs to be done. . . . If one seeks first and in a rational way righteousness and other eternal values—the essential content of the "Kingdom of God"—it promises that all he needs will be his, and that being rightly adjusted at the center of his life, he need not even be afraid of them that kill the body and after that have no more that they can do.[38]

Now it is significant that this statement of what moral optimism is uses the language of the gospels, and while the author founds this moral optimism upon universal reason he finds at the core of it certain of the principles of Jesus' teaching.[39] It designates precisely the attitude which Jesus taught. Jesus, however, expressed it in the simple religious terms of faith and love. In this moral optimism as designating man's fundamental attitude toward the universe we have another element of enduring value in Jesus' world-view. A similar evaluation is made by Baillie:

Neither in any earlier nor in any later teaching do we find an outlook on life suggested to us which is quite so convincingly true and right as the outlook set forth in the words and carried out in the deeds of the historic Jesus.[40]

As pointed out in Chapter V, the problem of evil constitutes the greatest problem which calls for solution in any world-view. Jesus faced this problem and found its solution in the principles of redemption, of heroic self-sacrifice, and of moral optimism.[41] He found its solution too in his profound inner assurance of the eternal value of righteousness and its ultimate triumph.

It was pointed out in Chapter VII that Jesus viewed life under the aspect of the eternal.[42] It was his view that the ethical principles he enunciated and stressed had ultimate survival value.[43] They would survive the passing away of the age in which he was himself living. They would survive the judgment. They would be valid when the ideal should be fully consummated and

[192]

eternal life in the kingdom of God should be an accomplished fact. Jesus' thinking was oriented toward the arrival of the ideal. His world-view has thus a quality of absoluteness about it. He did not formulate his ethical principles in the light of the most suitable adjustments that could be made to the existing order. Nor was his ethics an interim ethics, based upon the fears engendered by an imminent catastrophe.[44] Eternal interests and issues alone mattered to him.

Jesus did not advocate one type of religious living appropriate to the present as a mere preparation for the future, and portray a different type to characterize the age to come. . . . So far as the actual quality of the new life was concerned, expressed in terms of its attitudes, its motives, its ideals, and its sincerities, it was the same that Jesus would require now of those who strive to do the will of God.[45]

The place of apocalyptic in Jesus' world-view was acknowledged and expounded in Chapters V-VIII. Apocalyptic gave him the form in which he expressed his world-view. It did not affect the essence of his world-view in such a way that the passing of the apocalyptic mode of thought invalidated his philosophy of life. Jesus made the apocalyptic thought-form subserve his moral and spiritual ideas.

If any one element in the world-view of Jesus may be characterized as important above all else, it is this:

[193]

his thinking was oriented toward the eternal; his ethical judgments were formed on the basis of enduring values; he regarded the world and life *sub specie aeternitatis*. This determined his attitude toward both old and new. This principle applies both backwards and forwards. Jesus viewed the past of his people as preserved in the Jewish Scriptures under the eternal aspect and selected the best because he judged it to be of enduring value and put dynamic into it, and this because he first of all experienced that dynamic in his own soul. He viewed the age in which he lived under the aspect of the eternal. There was much about his own age that ought to and would pass away. It was the finest insight of Jesus that there were forces at work in his age making for the arrival of the ideal age. Upon these he threw all the weight of emphasis in teaching and endeavor in personal ministry.

This affords a basis for answering the modern problem: Is the teaching of Jesus of historical interest only, or does Jesus have any message valid for the present? The validity of Jesus' teaching for the present will be found where its validity for his own age and for his first followers was found, pertaining to those elements which are making for the arrival of the ethically and socially ideal. It is not in order in this connection to discuss the details of this modern problem. It is sufficient to point out the principle in Jesus' world-view to which it stands related. Jesus did consider that his teaching would be valid in the far-distant future because he thus viewed the universe and life in its eternal aspect and in his teaching aimed to set out those values which would endure when his own age had passed away and the eternal world-order of God's kingdom should be the ever-present order. Jesus did call upon his disciples to live the kingdom, i. e., the ideal, type of life in the age in which they lived however unideal that age was. He considered his ideal valid for that age and for any age to come because he deemed it eternally valid. He perceived an ideal world in the making. This is his philosophy of the world-process, his conception of the ultimate reality.

In the view of Jesus, God's immediate purpose is the establishment of this eternal order. Jesus regards God as actively at work now accomplishing this purpose. In popular Jewish thought, the locale of the messianic kingdom would be a regenerated earth. Jesus discerns God as already at work regenerating the earth. Jesus had nothing to say about the renewal or regeneration of outward nature. His concern was with the inner realm of man's nature, with moral renewal. He was in harmony with the prophets. Jeremiah set forth the promise of a new covenant:

[195]

This is the covenant that I will make with the house of Israel after those days, saith Yahweh: I will put my law in their inward parts, and in their heart will I write it; and I will be their God, and they shall be my people. And they shall teach no more every man his neighbor, and every man his brother, saying, Know Yahweh; for they shall all know me, from the least of them unto the greatest of them; saith Yahweh: for I will forgive their iniquity, and their sin will I remember no more.[46]

Ezekiel prophesied:

A new heart also will I give you, and a new spirit will I put within you; and I will take away the stony heart out of your flesh, and I will give you a heart of flesh. And I will put my Spirit within you, and cause you to walk in my statutes, and ye shall keep mine ordinances, and do them.[47]

Joel voiced the hope that God would pour out his Spirit on all flesh.[48] The Psalmist prays:

> Create in me a clean heart, O God;
> And renew a right spirit within me.[49]

The spiritual renewing of the people is the pronounced hope of Ps. Sol. 17.[50] This prophetic hope appears afresh in Jubilees:

And after this they will return to me in all uprightness and with their whole heart and with their whole soul, and I will circumcise the foreskin of their heart and the foreskin of the heart of their children, and I will create in them a holy spirit, and I will make them clean, so that they shall not turn away from me any more forever. And their souls will follow after me and after all my commandments, and they will fulfill my commandments, and I will be their Father and they will be my children. And they shall all be called children of the living God, and every angel and every spirit shall know it, and shall acknowledge that these are my children, and that I am their Father in truth and righteousness, and that I love them.[51]

It was Jesus' faith that this prophetic hope was being realized in his day, for God was at work ethically renewing man. As in other items of his world-view, he shaped his own practical activity in accordance with his philosophy. His own ministry of teaching was motivated by his consciousness of co-operating in this work of ethically renewing his people. Hence his message: "The kingdom of God is at hand: repent ye, and believe in the gospel."[52] Repentance and faith were the attitudes on man's part which were needed to release the divine powers that were at hand and achieve the ideal.

In its ultimate reach Jesus' ideal is a social ideal. It is the ideal of God and man in perfect society. Apparently Jesus could think of nothing beyond that. His teaching ministry was devoted to preparing men for participation in that divine society. This hope of a future coming of God's kingdom in which the ideal righteousness will be realized is a permanently valid incentive to human behavior. Jesus' view of the future was not an impossible Utopia. The thing that gives it its enduring value is the solid moral and religious substance on which it is grounded in his world-view, the ethical idealism which is the basal element in it. In present-day thought-form we may prefer to speak of the grand strategy of purposive evolution which moves toward the arrival of the fittest, or more poetically, to speak of the far-off divine event toward which the whole creation moves. Jesus did not view it as so far off, and expressed himself in simpler terms of religious faith: "Come, ye blessed of my Father, inherit the kingdom prepared for you from the foundation of the world."[53]

Chapter X

EPILOGUE: WISDOM INCARNATE

THE Jesus of history became the Christ of faith. Jesus stressed the principle of inwardness. The early·Christians applied this same principle to Jesus himself, and endeavored to interpret his person and his work. Jesus took the noblest and best which he found in man as a cue to his understanding of what God is like, on the view that God is not less than man at his best. In the parable of the lost son, Jesus portrayed human fatherhood in its aspect of seeking, redeeming love, meaning thereby that God as a Father is like that. God is giving and forgiving; giving, for "if ye, then, being evil, know how to give good gifts unto your children, how much more shall your Father who is in heaven give good things to them that ask him?"[1]; forgiving, "for we ourselves also forgive every one that is indebted to us."[2] The early Christians applied this same line of reasoning to Jesus himself as they sought to interpret his person and career, and they came to the view that God was like him. They thenceforth thought of God in terms of reference to him, "God the Father of our Lord Jesus Christ."[3] Jesus viewed life, and persons, and things *sub specie aeternitatis*. His followers viewed him in his eternal aspect and tried to state his relationship to the ultimate reality. The result was that the historical wisdom teacher became for the early Christian community the incarnate Wisdom of God.

The Jewish literature contains material which prepared their minds for such a thought-form. In the Jewish world-view, Wisdom was conceived as pre-existent. This is clearly set forth in Proverbs 8:22-31.

Yahweh formed me as the first of his works,
The beginning of his deeds of old;
In the earliest ages was I fashioned,
At the first when the earth began.
When there were no depths was I brought forth,
When there were no fountains brimming with water;
Before the mountains were sunk,
Before the hills was I brought forth;
While as yet he had not made the earth and the fields,
Nor the first clods of the world.
When he established the heavens I was there;
When he traced the vault over the face of the deep;
When he made firm the skies above,
When he fixed the fountains of the deep;
When he set for the sea its bound,
So that the waters should not transgress his commandment,
When he traced the foundations of the earth,
I was beside him as a ward of his;

And daily was I filled with delight,
I sported before him all the time—
Sported over this world of his—
Finding my delight in the sons of men.[4]

Wisdom not only was pre-existent, but became incarnate. This view is presented in two notable passages in the book of Sira (Ecclesiasticus).

Wisdom was created before them all, . . .
The Lord himself created her;
He saw her and counted her,
And poured her out upon all he made;
Upon all mankind, as he chose to bestow her;
But he supplied her liberally to those who loved him.[5]

I issued from the mouth of the Most High,
And covered the earth like a mist.
I lived on the heights,
And my throne was on the pillar of cloud.
I alone compassed the circuit of heaven,
And I walked in the depth of the abyss.
I owned the waves of the sea and the whole earth
And every people and nation.
Among all these I sought a resting-place;
In whose possession should I lodge?
Then the Creator of all gave me his command;
And he who created me made my tent rest,
And said, "Pitch your tent in Jacob,
And find your inheritance in Israel."
He created me from the beginning, before the world,
And I shall never cease.

I ministered before him in the holy tent,
And so was I established in Zion.
He made me rest likewise in the beloved city,
And I had authority over Jerusalem.
I took root in the glorified people,
In the portion of the Lord, and of his inheritance.[6]

The book of the Wisdom of Solomon presents a similar doctrine of Wisdom.

For wisdom, the fashioner of all things, taught me.[7]

For wisdom is more mobile than any motion,
And she penetrates and permeates everything, because she
    is so pure;
For she is the breath of the power of God,
And a pure emanation of his almighty glory;
Therefore nothing defiled can enter into her.
For she is a reflection of the everlasting light,
And a spotless mirror of the activity of God,
And a likeness of his goodness.
Though she is one, she can do all things,
And while remaining in herself, she makes everything new.
And passing into holy souls, generation after generation,
She makes them friends of God, and prophets.
For God loves nothing but the man who lives with wisdom.
For she is fairer than the sun,
Or any group of stars;
Compared with light, she is found superior;
For night succeeds to it,
But evil cannot overpower wisdom.
For she reaches in strength from one end of the earth to
    the other,
And conducts everything well.[8]

The conception that Wisdom would "pass into holy souls" is what gave rise to the doctrine of Jesus as the incarnate Wisdom of God. This Wisdom Christology is the Christology of that very early document, or ensemble of documents, to which we owe our knowledge of Jesus' teachings, namely, "Q," or the Second Source, as it is called by some. In interpreting Jesus as a wisdom teacher, in Chapter I, we cited Streeter's interpretation of "Q" as a collection of the "Wise Sayings" of Jesus.[9] The Wisdom Christology of "Q" is stated in the poem:

I thank thee, O Father, Lord of heaven and earth,
That thou didst hide these things from the wise and understanding,
And didst reveal them unto babes:
Yea, Father, for so it was well-pleasing in thy sight.

All things have been delivered unto me of my Father:
And no one knoweth the Son, save the Father;
Neither doth any know the Father, save the Son,
And he to whomsoever the Son willeth to reveal him.[10]

"Q" places in the mouth of Jesus the utterance of the "Wisdom of God":

Therefore also said the Wisdom of God, I will send unto them prophets and apostles (Matt., prophets, and wise men, and scribes); and some of them they shall kill and persecute.[11]

and follows this by the "Lament of Rejected Wisdom":

O Jerusalem, Jerusalem, that killeth the prophets, and

stoneth them that are sent unto her! how often would I have gathered thy children together, even as a hen gathereth her chickens under her wings, and ye would not! Behold, your house is left unto you desolate. For I say unto you, Ye shall not see me henceforth, till ye say, Blessed is he that cometh in the name of the Lord.[12]

"Q" represents Jesus as including John the Baptist among Wisdom's children in the remark: "Wisdom is justified of all her children."[13]

The Jewish tradition was one stream of influence that helped to shape the thinking of the early Christian community. Another line of influence was Greek thought. What the Jews called Wisdom, the Greeks called the Logos, i. e., Reason (commonly translated "Word"). The Logos was the creative effluence of God continuously coming into the world, uniting men with one another and with God.

This Greek doctrine of the Logos was appropriated by early Christianity and applied as a category of interpretation to Christ in the prologue to the Fourth Gospel.

In the beginning was the Logos,
And the Logos was with God,
And the Logos was God.

The same was in the beginning with God.
All things were made through him;
And without him was not anything made that hath been made.

In him was life,
And the life was the light of men.
And the light shineth in the darkness,
And the darkness apprehended it not. . . .

There was the true light,
Even the light which lighteth every man,
Coming into the world.

He was in the world,
And the world was made through him,
And the world knew him not.

He came unto his own,
And they that were his own received him not.
But as many as received him,
To them gave he the right to become children of God. . . .

And the Logos became flesh,
And dwelt among us, . . .
Full of grace and truth. . . .

For of his fulness we all received,
And grace for grace.
For the law was given through Moses,
Grace and truth came through Jesus Christ.

No man hath seen God at any time;
The only begotten Son, who is in the bosom of the Father,
He hath declared him.[14]

Both the Jewish and the Greek lines of influence

helped to shape the apostle Paul's thinking about Christ. Paul expressed his view as follows:

[Christ] is the image of the invisible God, the firstborn of all creation; for in him were all things created, in the heavens and upon the earth, things visible and things invisible, whether thrones or dominions or principalities or powers; all things have been created through him, and unto him; and he is before all things, and in him all things consist.[15]

Paul also spoke of "Christ the power of God, and the wisdom of God;"[16] of "Christ Jesus, who was made unto us wisdom from God;"[17] of "Christ, in whom are all the treasures of wisdom and knowledge hidden."[18]

The New Testament Epistle to the Hebrews employed the same Wisdom Christology:

God, having of old time spoken unto the fathers in the prophets by divers portions and in divers manners, hath at the end of these days spoken unto us in his Son, whom he appointed heir of all things, through whom also he made the worlds; who being the effulgence of his glory, and the very image of his substance, and upholding all things by the word of his power, when he had made purification of sins, sat down on the right hand of the Majesty on high.[19]

The Wisdom Christology was, of course, not the only type of Christology, but it was one type, and it greatly influenced Christian thinking. It influenced St. Paul profoundly. He spoke of Christ, "Whom we proclaim, admonishing every man and teaching every man in all wisdom, that we may present every man perfect in Christ."[20] He spoke of "bringing every thought into captivity to the obedience of Christ."[21] Paul employed the Wisdom Christology especially in his letter to the Colossians, from which we have presented three quotations in this context. He exhorted the Colossian Christians to "let the inspiration of Christ dwell in your midst with all its wealth of wisdom,"[22] and to "let Christian wisdom rule your behavior to the outside world."[23] And a second-century Christian author expressed the noble sentiment: "Blessed are they that receive the wisdom of Jesus Christ, for they shall be called sons of the Most High."[24]

BIBLIOGRAPHY

ABBREVIATIONS

APOT. *The Apocrypha and Pseudepigrapha of the Old Testament.* Ed. by Robert Henry Charles. 2 vols. Oxford, Clarendon Press. 1913.

DB. *A Dictionary of the Bible.* Ed. by James Hastings. 5 vols. N. Y., Scribner. 1911.

DB (one vol. ed.). *Dictionary of the Bible,* one volume edition. Ed. by James Hastings. N. Y., Scribner. 1921.

DCG. *Dictionary of Christ and the Gospels.* Ed. by James Hastings. N. Y., Scribner. 1909.

EB. *Encyclopaedia Biblica.* Ed. by T. K. Cheyne and J. Sutherland. 4 vols. N. Y., Macmillan. 1899-1903.

ERE. *Encyclopaedia of Religion and Ethics.* Ed. by James Hastings. 13 vols. N. Y., Scribner. 1908-1927.

Exp. *Expositor.* Ed. (1885-   ) by U. R. Nicoll. London, Hodder and Stoughton. 1875—.

ICC. *International Critical Commentary.* N. Y., Scribner. 1899—.

JBL. *Journal of Biblical Literature.* New Haven, Society of Biblical Literature and Exegesis. 1881—.

JE. *Jewish Encyclopaedia.* Ed. by Isidore Singer. 12 vols. N. Y., Funk and Wagnalls. 1901.

JQR. *Jewish Quarterly Review.* Ed. by I. Abrahams and C. G. Montefiore. London. 1888-1908.

BIBLIOGRAPHY

JR. *Journal of Religion*. Chicago, University of Chicago
  Press. 1921—.
RV. *The Holy Bible, The American Standard Version*.
  N. Y., Nelson. 1901.
WH. *The New Testament in the Original Greek*. By B. F.
  Westcott and F. J. A. Hort. London, Macmillan.
  1907.

Selected Books of Reference

Abrahams, Israel. *Studies in Pharisaism and the Gospels*.
  First Series. Cambridge. 1917.
Ames, Edward Scribner. *Religion*. N. Y., Holt. 1929.
Angus, Samuel. *The Mystery Religions and Christianity*.
  N. Y., Scribner. 1925.
Bacon, Benjamin Wisner. *The Gospel of the Hellenists*.
  N. Y., Holt. 1933.
Bacon, Benjamin Wisner. *He Opened to Us the Scriptures*.
  N. Y., Macmillan. 1923.
Bacon, Benjamin Wisner. *Jesus and Paul*. N. Y., Macmillan.
  1921.
Bacon, Benjamin Wisner. *Jesus the Son of God*. N. Y., Holt.
  1930.
Bacon, Benjamin Wisner. *The Story of Jesus*. N. Y., Scrib-
  ner. 1927.
Bacon, Benjamin Wisner. *Studies in Matthew*. N. Y., Holt.
  1930.
Baillie, John. *The Interpretation of Religion*. N. Y., Scrib-
  ner. 1929.
Baillie, John. *The Place of Jesus Christ in Modern Chris-
  tianity*. N. Y., Scribner. 1929.
Barton, George Aaron. *Ecclesiastes*. ICC. N. Y., Scribner.
  1908.

[209]

Barton, George Aaron. *The Religions of the World*. Chicago, University of Chicago Press. 1919.

Barton, George Aaron. *Studies in New Testament Christianity*. Philadelphia. 1928.

Bertholet, D. A. *Die Jüdische Religion von der Zeit Esras bis zum Zeitalter Christi*. Tübingen. 1911.

Bosworth, Edward Increase. *The Life and Teachings of Jesus*. N. Y., Macmillan. 1924.

Bousset, Johann Franz Wilhelm. *Jesus*. N. Y., Putnam. 1911.

Branscomb, Bennett Harvie. *The Teachings of Jesus*. Nashville, Cokesbury. 1931.

Bultmann, Rudolf. *Jesus*. Berlin. 1926. Eng. tr.: *Jesus and the Word*. N. Y., Scribner. 1934.

Bundy, Walter Ernest. *Our Recovery of Jesus*. Indianapolis, Bobbs Merrill. 1929.

Bundy, Walter Ernest. *The Religion of Jesus*. Indianapolis, Bobbs Merrill. 1928.

Burch, Ernest Ward. *The Ethical Teaching of the Gospels*. N. Y., Abingdon. 1925.

Burton, Ernest DeWitt. *Christianity in the Modern World*. Ed. by H. R. Willoughby. Chicago, University of Chicago Press. 1927.

Burton, Ernest DeWitt. *Spirit, Soul and Flesh*. Chicago, University of Chicago Press. 1918.

Burton, Ernest DeWitt. *The Teaching of Jesus, A Source Book*. Chicago, University of Chicago Press. 1924.

Buttrick, George Arthur. *The Parables of Jesus*. N. Y., Doubleday, Doran. 1928.

Cadbury, Henry Joel. *The Peril of Modernizing Jesus*. N. Y., Macmillan. 1937.

BIBLIOGRAPHY

Cadoux, Arthur Temple. *The Parables of Jesus*. N. Y., Macmillan. 1931.

Case, Shirley Jackson. *Experience with the Supernatural in Early Christian Times*. N. Y., Century. 1929.

Case, Shirley Jackson. *Jesus, A New Biography*. Chicago, University of Chicago Press. 1927.

Charles, Robert Henry. *The Book of Enoch*. Oxford, Clarendon Press. 1912.[2]

Charles, Robert Henry. *A Critical History of the Doctrine of a Future Life*. Cited as *Eschatology*. London. 1913.[2]

Charles, Robert Henry. *Religious Development Between the Old and New Testaments*. N. Y., Holt. 1914.

Davidson, A. B. *Biblical and Literary Essays*. N. Y., Armstrong. 1902.

Deissmann, Adolf. *Paul, A Study in Social and Religious History*. London, Hodder and Stoughton. 1926.

Deissmann, Adolf. *The Religion of Jesus and the Faith of Paul*. N. Y., Doran. 1923.

Denny, Walter Bell. *The Career and Significance of Jesus*. N. Y., Nelson. 1933.

Derwacter, Frederick Milton. *Preparing the Way for Paul*. N. Y., Macmillan. 1930.

Dibelius, Martin. *From Tradition to Gospel*. N. Y., Scribner. 1935.

Dill, Samuel. *Roman Society from Nero to Marcus Aurelius*. London, Macmillan. 1905.

Dodd, Charles Harold. *The Parables of the Kingdom*. N. Y., Scribner. 1936.

Easton, Burton Scott. *What Jesus Taught*. N. Y., Abingdon. 1938.

Fairweather, William. *The Background of the Gospels, or*

Judaism in the Period Between the Old and New Testaments. Edinburgh, Clark. 1920.[3]

Fosdick, Harry Emerson. *A Guide to Understanding the Bible.* N. Y., Harper. 1938.

Friedlander, Gerald. *Hellenism and Christianity.* London, Routledge. 1912.

Gilbert, George Holley. *The Interpretation of the Bible, A Short History.* N. Y., Macmillan. 1908.

Glover, Terrot Reaveley. *The Jesus of History.* N. Y., Association Press. 1917.

Goguel, Maurice. *The Life of Jesus.* N. Y., Macmillan. 1933.

Goodspeed, Edgar Johnson. *The Apocrypha, An American Translation.* Chicago, University of Chicago Press. 1938.

Goodspeed, Edgar Johnson. *Introduction to the New Testament.* Chicago, University of Chicago Press. 1937.

Goodspeed, Edgar Johnson. *The New Testament, An American Translation.* Chicago, University of Chicago Press. 1923.

Graham, William Creighton. *The Prophets and Israel's Culture.* Chicago, University of Chicago Press. 1934.

Grant, Frederick C. *The Gospel of the Kingdom.* N. Y., Macmillan. 1940.

Guignebert, Charles Alfred Honoré. *Jesus.* N. Y., Knopf. 1935.

Guignebert, Charles Alfred Honoré. *The Jewish World in the Time of Jesus.* London, Routledge. 1939.

Headlam, Arthur C. *The Life and Teaching of Jesus the Christ.* London, Oxford. 1923.

Herford, R. Travers. *Judaism in the New Testament Period.* London, Lindsay. 1929.

BIBLIOGRAPHY

Herford, R. Travers. *The Pharisees*. N. Y., Macmillan. 1924.

Hicks, R. D. *Stoic and Epicurean*. N. Y., Scribner. 1910.

Horne, Herman Harrel. *Jesus as a Philosopher*. N. Y., Abingdon. 1927.

Kent, Charles Foster. *The Sermons, Epistles and Apocalypses of Israel's Prophets*. N. Y., Scribner. 1910.

Kent, Charles Foster. *The Wise Men of Ancient Israel and Their Proverbs*. N. Y., Silver, Burdett. 1895.

King, L. W. *The Seven Tablets of Creation*. London, Luzac. 1902.

Klausner, Joseph. *Jesus of Nazareth*. N. Y., Macmillan. 1925.

Lake, Kirsopp. *Landmarks of Early Christianity*. London. 1920.

Ligon, Ernest Mayfield. *The Psychology of Christian Personality*. N. Y., Macmillan. 1935.

McCown, Chester Charlton. *The Genesis of the Social Gospel*. N. Y., Knopf. 1929.

Macintosh, Douglas Clyde. *The Reasonableness of Christianity*. N. Y., Scribner. 1925.

Macintosh, Douglas Clyde. *Social Religion*. N. Y., Scribner. 1939.

Mackinnon, James. *The Historic Jesus*. N. Y., Longmans, Green. 1931.

Mahaffy, John Pentland. *The Progress of Hellenism in Alexander's Empire*. Chicago. 1905.

Manson, Thomas Walter. *The Teaching of Jesus*. Cambridge. 1931.

Mathews, Shailer. *Jesus on Social Institutions*. N. Y., Macmillan. 1928.

[213]

Mathews, Shailer. *New Testament Times in Palestine.* N. Y., Macmillan. 1934.

Moffatt, James. *An Introduction to the Literature of the New Testament.* N. Y., Scribner. 1911.

Moffatt, James. *The Holy Bible, Containing the Old and New Testaments, A New Translation.* N. Y., Doran. 1926.

Montefiore, Claude G. *Some Elements of the Religious Teaching of Jesus.* N. Y., Macmillan. 1910.

Montefiore, Claude G. *The Synoptic Gospels.* 2 vols. London, Macmillan. 1927.[2]

Moore, George Foot. *Judaism in the First Century of the Christian Era: The Age of the Tannaim.* Cambridge, Mass., Harvard University Press. 1927.

Morfill, W. R., and Charles, R. H. *The Book of the Secrets of Enoch.* Oxford. 1896.

Mould, Elmer Wallace King. *Essentials of Bible History.* N. Y., Nelson. 1939.

Porter, Frank Chamberlain. *The Messages of the Apocalyptical Writers.* N. Y., Scribner. 1905.

Porter, Frank Chamberlain. *The Mind of Christ in Paul.* N. Y., Scribner. 1930.

Rawlinson, Alfred Edward John. *The Gospel According to Mark.* London, Methuen. 1925.

Rawlinson, Alfred Edward John. *The New Testament Doctrine of the Christ.* London, Longmans, Green. 1926.

Robinson, Benjamin Willard. *The Sayings of Jesus.* N. Y., Harper. 1930.

Robinson, H. Wheeler. *The Christian Doctrine of Man.* Edinburgh. 1911.

Robinson, Willard Haskell. *The Parables of Jesus.* Chicago, University of Chicago Press. 1928.

Scott, A. Boyd. *Christ: The Wisdom of Man*. London, Hodder and Stoughton. 1928.

Scott, Charles Archibald Anderson. *New Testament Ethics*. N. Y., Macmillan. 1930.

Scott, Ernest Findlay. *The Ethical Teaching of Jesus*. N. Y., Macmillan. 1934.

Scott, Ernest Findlay. *The Gospel and Its Tributaries*. Edinburgh. 1929.

Scott, Ernest Findlay. *The Kingdom and the Messiah*. Edinburgh. 1911.

Scott, Ernest Findlay. *The Kingdom of God in the New Testament*. N. Y., Macmillan. 1931.

Scott, Ernest Findlay. *The Literature of the New Testament*. N. Y., Columbia University Press. 1932.

Slaten, A. Wakefield. *What Jesus Taught*. Chicago, University of Chicago Press. 1922.

Smith, John Merlin Powis, Editor. *The Old Testament, An American Translation*. Chicago, University of Chicago Press. 1927.

Stevens, George Barker. *The Teaching of Jesus*. N. Y., Macmillan. 1902.

Strack, Hermann L. and Billerbeck, Paul. *Kommentar zum Neuen Testament aus Talmud und Midrash*. 3 vols. München, Beck. 1922.

Streeter, Burnett Hillman. *The Four Gospels*. N. Y., Macmillan. 1925.

Tittle, Ernest Fremont. *Jesus After Nineteen Centuries*. N. Y., Abingdon. 1932.

Walker, Thomas. *The Teaching of Jesus and the Jewish Teaching of His Age*. N. Y., Doran. 1923.

Weigle, Luther Allan. *Jesus and the Educational Method*. N. Y., Abingdon. 1939.

Weinel, Heinrich. *Biblische Theologie des Neuen Testaments*. Tübingen. 1928.[4]

Weinel, Heinrich. *St. Paul, the Man and his Work*. N. Y., Putnam. 1906.

Weiss, Johannes. *Paul and Jesus*. London, Harper. 1909.

Wendt, Hans Hinrich. *Die Begriffe Fleisch und Geist*. Gotha. 1878.

Wendt, Hans Hinrich. *The Teaching of Jesus*. 2 vols. N. Y., Scribner. 1899.

Wernle, Paul. *Jesus*. Tübingen. 1917.

Wicks, Henry J. *The Doctrine of God in Jewish Apocryphal and Apocalyptic Literature*. London, Hunter and Longhurst. 1915.

Wilder, Amos Niven. *Eschatology and Ethics in the Teaching of Jesus*. N. Y., Harper. 1939.

NOTES AND REFERENCES

CHAPTER I

1. Matt. 23:34 distinguishes prophets, wise men, and scribes; scribes here clearly means legalistic scribes, i. e., lawyers. 2. C. H. Toy, "Wisdom Literature," EB, iv, 5325. 3. Jer. 8:8; 9:23; 18:18. Cf. Isa. 29:14. 4. Prov. 22:17-24:22. Cf. M. H. Dunsmore, "An Egyptian Contribution to the Book of Proverbs," JR, v (1925), pp. 300-308, *in re* "The Admonitions of Amenepotet." 5. Wm. Fairweather, *The Background of the Gospels or Judaism in the Period Between the Old and New Testaments,* 1920,[3] Edinburgh, p. 82. 6. Cf. A. R. Gordon, "Wisdom," ERE, xii, p. 746b. 7. Job 28:12. 8. Job 28:13a. 9. Job 28:21a. 10. Job 28:23a. 11. Job 28:28b. 12. Prov. 30:1-9. 13. Vs. 4. 14. Vss. 7f. 15. Eccl. 12:13. 16. A. B. Davidson, *Biblical and Literary Essays,* N. Y., 1902, p. 32. 17. Heinrich Weinel, *St. Paul, the Man and his Work,* N. Y., 1906, p. 8. 18. Aboth 1:17. 19. Ernest DeWitt Burton, *Christianity in the Modern World,* ed. by H. R. Willoughby, Chicago, 1927, pp. 11-26. 20. Maurice Goguel, *The Life of Jesus,* N. Y., 1933, p. 212. 21. Hans Hinrich Wendt, *Die Lehre Jesu,* Göttingen, 1901,[2] p. 137. 22. Job, Proverbs, and Ecclesiastes. 23. So C. F. Kent, *The Wise Men of Ancient Israel and their Proverbs,* N. Y., 1895. 24. Alfred Plummer, *Exp.* 7th series, vol. 6 (Dec. 1908), p. 482; W. F. Adeney, DCG, i, 101a; Jas. Moffatt, *Introduction,* p. 26. 25. Cf. B. W. Bacon, *He Opened to Us the Scriptures,* N. Y., 1923, p. 61. 26. *Religious Development Between the Old and the New Testaments,* N. Y., 1914. 27. Test. Gad 6. Cf. Lk. 17:3; Matt. 18:15, 35. 28. R. H. Charles, *op. cit.,* p. 156. 29. Antonin Causse, *Les "pauvres" d'Israel (prophètes, psalmistes, messianistes),* Strasbourg-Paris: Istra, 1922, p. 139; cf. C. C. McCown, *The Genesis of the Social Gospel,* N. Y., 1929, p. 290. 30. Lk. 2:41-51. 31. Vs. 47. 32. Vs. 52. 33. Cf. R. T. Herford, *Judaism in the New Testament Period,* London, 1928, p. 147. 34. Lk. 4:16. 35. For a description of the synagogue services, see Herford, *op. cit.,* pp. 161-173. 36. Cf. I. Abrahams, *Studies in Pharisaism and the Gospels,* Cambridge, 1917, i, 10. 37. Abrahams, *op. cit.,* p. 4. 38. Herford, *Judaism,* etc., p. 193. 39. *Ibid.,* p. 194. 40. Cf. B. W. Bacon, *He Opened to Us the Scriptures,* N. Y., 1923, pp.

69-73 on Jesus' personal study of the Scriptures. 41. H. H. Wendt, *The Teaching of Jesus*, N. Y., 1899, ii, 3-5, enumerates details of Jesus' intimate knowledge of the Old Testament. 42. Lev. 19:18. Cf. Mk. 12:31 = Matt. 22:39 = Lk. 10:27. 43. Matt. 13:52. 44. Matt. 18:22. 45. Gen. 4:24. 46. Mk. 12:26f. = Matt. 22:31f. = Lk. 20:37f. 47. Mk. 2:23-28 = Matt. 12:1-8 = Lk. 6:1-5. 48. Mk. 10:2-9 = Matt. 19:3-8. 49. E. g., Gen. 1:27; 2:24; 5:2. 50. Ernest DeWitt Burton, *loc. cit.*, p. 17. 51. Matt. 5:17. 52. H. H. Wendt, *op. cit*, ii, 15. 53. Amos N. Wilder, *Eschatology and Ethics in the Teaching of Jesus*, N. Y., 1939, p. 150. 54. Sir. 39:1-10. Quoted from E. J. Goodspeed, *The Apocrypha, An American Translation*, Chicago, 1938. 55. Prov. 1:20ff.; 8:2ff. 56. Prov. 1:20ff. Translation by A. R. Gordon in *The Old Testament, An American Translation*, ed. by J. M. P. Smith, Chicago, 1927. 57. Prov. 8:1-5. Translation by A. R. Gordon in *The Old Testament, An American Translation*, ed. by J. M. P. Smith, Chicago, 1927. 58. Sir. 51:23. Translation by Box and Oesterley. 59. Sir. 6:36. Translation by Box and Oesterley. 60. Ab. 1:4. 61. Prov. 13:20. 62. Lk. 2:52. 63. It is surprising that even such a recent book as L. A. Weigle's *Jesus and the Educational Method*, N. Y., 1939, devoted as it is to emphasizing the fact that Jesus was a teacher, totally ignores the educational method of those historic Jewish teachers of wisdom who were the real educators of the time. 64. C. W. Votaw, in an academic lecture, "New Testament Ethics," University of Chicago, July 17, 1928. 65. C. F. Kent, *op. cit.*, p. 30. 65a. Jn. 13:13. 66. Mk. 1:38. 67. Mk. 4:1-34; 10; 13. 68. Mk. 9:5; 11:21; 14:45; Rabboni in Mk. 10:51; cf. Jn. 20:16; the Greek equivalent form *didaskale* occurs in Mk. 4:38; 9:38; 10:35; 13:1. 69. Mk. 6:56; cf. Matt. 9:20; 14:36; 23:5; Lk. 8:44. Cf. B. W. Bacon, *The Story of Jesus*, N. Y., 1927, p. 209. 70. B. H. Streeter, *The Four Gospels*, N. Y., 1925, p. 286. 71. Rudolf Bultmann, "The New Approach to the Synoptic Problem," JR, vi (1926), p. 356. 72. *Ibid*. p. 360. 73. John Baillie, *The Place of Jesus Christ in Modern Christianity*, N. Y., 1929, p. 65. 74. Matt. 11:7-19 = Lk. 7:24-35. 75. Lk. 7:35. Cf. Matt. 11:19, reading *teknōn* with CDLXΘal pler. 76. Cf. H. Weinel, *Biblische Theologie des Neuen Testaments*, 1921,[3] p. 122. 77. Lk. 11:49. Cf. Moffatt's note, *Introduction*, p. 33. 78. Matt. 23:34. 79. Matt. 11:28-30. 80. Sir. 6:23-31. Quoted from E. J. Goodspeed, *The Apocrypha, An American Translation*. Chicago, 1938. 81. Matt. 11:25-27 = Lk. 10:21f. This passage is ably discussed by G. A. Barton in "The Mysticism of Jesus," in *At One With the Invisible*, ed. by E. H. Sneath, N. Y., 1921, pp. 73-76. 82. B. W. Bacon, *Jesus and Paul*, N. Y., 1921, p. 186. 83. Matt. 23:37 = Lk. 13:34. 84. Lk. 13:26. 85. Mk. 6:1f. 86. Matt. 13:54. 87. Lk. 4:22. 88. Mk. 6:34. 89. Herford, *Judaism Etc.*, pp. 73, 195. 90. Cf. S. J. Case, *Jesus—A New Biography*, Chicago, 1927, p. 291. 91. *Vid. infra*, Chapter

8, pp. 170ff. 92. Cf. F. M. Derwacter, *Preparing the Way for Paul*, N. Y., 1930. 93. Cf. Samuel Dill, *Roman Society from Nero to Marcus Aurelius*, N. Y., 1905, pp. 340-342. 94. Cf. R. D. Hicks, *Stoic and Epicurean*, N. Y., 1910, p. 54. 95. Discourses, III, 22 gives a description of the Cynic-Stoic teacher. 96. R. M. Wenley, "Neo-Cynicism," ERE, ix, 298. 97. John P. Mahaffy, *The Progress of Hellenism in Alexander's Empire*, Chicago, 1905, p. 97. 98. The synoptic gospels represent Jesus as sending out his disciples as itinerant preachers. Mk. 6:6b-11; Matt. 9:35-10:1,5-16; Lk. 9:1-5; cf. Lk. 10:1-12. 99. A. Boyd Scott, *Christ, the Wisdom of Man*, London, 1928, p. 302.

CHAPTER II

1. Cf. Stephen Herbert Langdon, *Semitic Mythology*, Boston, 1931, pp. 216-218, for diagram and discussion of a Babylonian clay-tablet map of the world, ca. 2000 B.C. 2. Cf. D. A. Bertholet, *Die jüdische Religion von der Zeit Esras bis zum Zeitalter Christi*, Tübingen, 1911, pp. 127-133, *in re* "Welt- und Himmelsbild in Hiobbuch." 3. Job 26:10; Isa. 40:22; cf. Ps. 136:6; Isa. 40:28; 42:5; 44:24. 4. Job 28:24; Isa. 40:28. 5. Isa. 11:12. 6. I Sam. 2:8; Prov. 8:29; Ps. 18:16; 24:2; 75:3; 93:1; 104:5. 7. Job 9:6. 8. Ps. 46:3; Judith 16:15. 9. Job 38:6. 10. Job 26:7. 11. Job 38:18. 12. Job 26:10. 13. Job 38:8-11. 14. *Ibid.* 15. Gen. 7:11; 8:2; Jub. 5:24. 16. Jub. 8:12. 17. Dan. 11:16, 41, 45; I En. 27:1; 28:40. 18. Jub. 13:6. 19. Jub. 8:19; I En. 26:1. 20. Cf. Wm. Bacher, *Die Agada der Tannaiten*, Strassburg, 1903,[2] i, 371. 21. Jub. 8:19. 22. Cf. Bertholet, *op. cit.*, p. 398. 23. I En. 17:2; 18:8. Cf. the "mountain of God" in Ezk. 28:14, 16; Isa. 14:13; and the "exceeding high mountain" of the temptation narrative, Matt. 4:8. 24. I En. 18:6-10; 24:1-3; 32:1; 77:4. 25. I En. 77:5f. 26. I En. 77:8. 27. III Bar. 2. Cf. I En. 18:14; 33:1f.; 65:2; 76:1. 28. I En. 18:1. 29. Ps. 24:2; Gen. 1:2. 30. Gen. 1:21. 31. Job 9:13; 26:12; Ps. 89:10; Isa. 51:9. 32. Job 3:8; 40:5-41:26; Ps. 74:14; 104:26; Isa. 27:1; I. En. 60:7. 33. Amos 9:3. 34. Job 11:8; Ps. 139:8; and numerously. 35. Prov. 2:19. 36. Job 26:6; 28:22; 31:12. 37. Job 38:17. 38. Gen. 7:11; 8:2. Cf. I En. 54:7-9. 39. I En. 10:6, 13; 21:7-10; 90:24; IV Ezr. 5:8. 40. I En. 17:5. 41. I En. 22:9. 42. Job 38:17; 17:16. On the latter cf. note in *The Old Testament, An American Translation*, ed. by J. M. P. Smith, p. 1660; also Bertholet, *op. cit.*, p. 127. Cf. Matt. 16:18 on the "gates of Hades." 43. Gen. 1:6. 44. Gen. 1:7; Ps. 148:4. 45. Ps. 104:2; Isa. 40:22. 46. Isa. 34:4; Sib. Orac. 3:82. 47. Job 37:18. 48. I En. 18:10, 14; 71:4; 75:5. 49. Job 26:11. 50. Job 26:9. 51. Ps. 11:4; 103:19; Isa. 66:1. Cf. Moses' vision in Ex. 24:10 of "a paved work of sapphire stone" under the feet of the "God of Israel;" and Ezekiel's vision (1:22, 26) of the firmament sup-

porting the throne of God. Cf. Job 22:14, "He walketh upon the vault of heaven." 52. As there are the levitical singers in the Jerusalem temple, so there are the "sons of the gods" (Ps. 29:1) in heaven. 53. Job 38:33; Jer. 33:25. Cf. Ps. 148:6. 54. Ps. 89:36f.; 104:19. 55. Ps. 104:19; Sir. 43:6-8. 56. Job 38:7. *Sic contra* Gen. 1. 57. Jgs. 5:20; Job 37:9; 38:28f. 58. Job 36:29. Cf. 38:27; 37:16. 59. Job 38:22; cf. vs. 37, "God tilts the waterskins of the heavens," (*The Old Testament, An American Translation,* in loc.). I En. 41:4; 69:23. Other mention of atmospheric store chambers in I En. 11:1; 17:3; 41:4; 60:19ff.; 69:23; IV Ezr. 6:40; II Bar. 10:11; 59:11. 60. Ps. 78:26; 135:7; Jer. 10:13; 51:16. 61. I En. 18:1; 41:4; 60:12. 62. I En. 34:1-36:2; 76. 63. Job 28:25; I En. 60:12; II Bar. 59:5. 64. Job 28:26; 38:25. 65. Gen. 7:11; 8:2; I En. 101:2. 66. I En. 72f.; 75:3f.; II En. 11:2; cf. II Kgs. 6:17; 23:11. 67. I En. 33:3; 36:3; II En. 13:1. 68. I En. 72:3. 69. 13:2. 70. II En. 14:3. 71. I En. 72:5; 78:5. 72. I En. 72:4. 73. I En. 72:37; 78:3. 74. I En. 72:37; 73:3; cf. Isa. 30:26. 75. Gen. 1:14; I En. 75:3; 82:9-20. 76. Ps. 148:4. 77. Cf. II Cor. 12:2, 4. Apoc. Mos. 37 mentions third heaven. 78. III Bar. 2-16. 79. T. Levi 2-3; Ascen. Isa. 7-11. 80. II En. 3-22. 81. R. H. Charles, *The Apocrypha and Pseudepigrapha of the Old Testament,* ii, 305f. 82. Chaps. 3-6. 83. Chap. 7. 84. Chaps. 8, 10, 85. Chaps. 11-14. 86. Chap. 17. 87. Chap. 18. 88. Chap. 19. 89. Chap. 20. On this whole conception see R. H. Charles in Morfill and Charles, *The Book of the Secrets of Enoch,* Oxford, 1896, esp. pp. xxxvi-xxxviii. 90. Matt. 11:25 = Lk. 10:21. 91. Mk. 4:1-9 = Matt. 13:1-9 = Lk. 8:4-8. 92. Mk. 4:26-29. 93. Lk. 6:48f. = Matt. 7:25-27. 94. Lk. 12:56 = Matt. 16:3 (double bracketed in WH). 95. Matt. 12:42 = Lk. 11:31. 96. Mk. 13:27 = Matt. 24:31. 97. Matt. 5:34f. 98. Matt. 6:10. 99. "Father, who is in heaven," or "heavenly Father": Matt. 5:16; Mk. 11:25, cf. Matt. 6:14; Matt. 5:45, 48; 6:1, 9, 26 (cf. Lk. 12:24), 32 (cf. Lk. 12:30); Matt. 7:11 (cf. Lk. 11:13), 21; 10:32, 33; 12:50; 15:13; 16:17; 18:10, 14, 19, 35; 23:9. 100. Matt. 5:34; 23:22. 101. Matt. 18:10; Mk. 13:32 = Matt. 24:36; Mk. 12:25 = Matt. 22:30. Cf. Lk. 20:36. 102. Mk. 13:24, 25, 26; 14:62; Matt. 24:29, 30; 26:64; Lk. 21:11, 25, 26, 27. 103. Mk. 13:31; cf. Matt. 24:35 and Lk. 21:33; Matt. 5:17; cf. Lk. 16:17. 104. In the following passages the expression is put into the mouth of Jesus: 4:17; 5:3, 10, 19, 20; 7:21; 8:11; 10:7; 11:11, 12; 13:11, 24, 31, 33, 44, 45, 47, 52; 16:19; 18:3, 4, 23; 19:12, 14, 23; 20:1; 22:2; 23:13; 25:1, 14. Cf. S. J. Case, *Jesus—A New Biography,* p. 244, note 1. 105. Mk. 11:30-32 = Matt. 21:25-26 = Lk. 20:4-6. 106. Lk. 10:15 = Matt. 11:23. 107. Lk. 16:19-31. 108. *Supra,* p. 37. 109. II En. 8, 10; *vid. supra,* p. 40. 110. See H. H. Wendt, *The Teaching of Jesus,* i, pp. 168-170. 111. 23:43. 112. See L. W. King, *The Seven Tablets of Creation,* London, 1902, vol. i, p. xcv. 113. Mk. 10:6 = Matt. 19:4, 8. 114. Lk. 11:50. 115. Mk. 13:19. Cf. Matt.

24:21, "from the beginning of the world." 116. Matt. 25:34. 117. Prov. 3:19. Translation by A. R. Gordon in *The Old Testament, An American Translation,* ed. by J. M. P. Smith, Chicago, 1927; altering LORD = Yahweh. 118. Ps. 104:24. 119. Prov. 8:22-31. Translation by A. R. Gordon, *loc. cit.;* altering LORD = Yahweh. 120. Job 28:20-28. Translation by J. M. P. Smith in *The Old Testament, An American Translation,* Chicago, 1927. 121. Sir. 1:1-2, 8-9. 122. Sir. 1:1-4a. 123. Sir. 24:9. 124. Sir. 24:3-6a. 125. Sir. 24:6b-11. 126. *Supra,* p. 8. 127. Mk. 10:27 = Matt. 19:26 = Lk. 18:27. 128. A. Boyd Scott, *Christ: The Wisdom of Man.* London, 1928, p. 297. 129. Matt. 6:28 = Lk. 12:27. 130. Mk. 13:28 = Matt. 24:32 = Lk. 21:30. 131. Matt. 11:7 = Lk. 7:24. 132. Matt. 8:20 = Lk. 9:58. 133. Mk. 4:32 = Matt. 13:32 = Lk. 13:19. 134. Matt. 6:26 = Lk. 12:24. 135. Matt. 24:28 = Lk. 17:37. 136. Matt. 23:37 = Lk. 13:34. 137. Matt. 10:16; cf. Lk. 10:3. 138. *Ibid.* 139. Matt. 8:20 = Lk. 9:58. 140. Matt. 7:6. 141. Matt. 7:15. 142. Matt. 10:16 = Lk. 10:3. 143. Matt. 5:13 = Mk. 9:50b = Lk. 14:34b, 35a. 144. Matt. 5:14. 145. Mk. 2:21f. = Matt. 9:16f. = Lk. 5:37f. 146. Matt. 5:45. 147. Mk. 4:26-29. 148. Mk. 4:30-32 = Matt. 13:31-32 = Lk. 13:18, 19. 149. Matt. 13:33 = Lk. 13:20, 21. 150. Matt. 13:24-30. 151. G. B. Stevens, *The Teaching of Jesus,* N. Y., 1902, p. 119. 152. Cf. his statement on "The Growth of Science," in *New York Times,* June 26, 1939. 153. Cf. G. B. Stevens, *op. cit.,* pp. 119, 129; and H. H. Wendt, *The Teaching of Jesus,* pp. 152, 167f., 171f. 154. Job, chaps. 38-41. 155. Mk. 4:11 = Matt. 13:11 = Lk. 8:10. 156. Cf. B. W. Bacon, *The Story of Jesus,* p. 212. 157. D. C. Macintosh, *The Reasonableness of Christianity,* N. Y., 1925, p. 87.

CHAPTER III

1. Gen. 1:26f. 2. Gen. 2:7. 3. Gen. 1:24-30. 4. RVmarg. 5. Cf. James Orr, "Image," DB (one vol. ed.), p. 377. 6. Gen. 1:27. 7. Mk. 10:6 = Lk. 19:4. 8. I Cor. 6:19; cf. II Cor. 5:4, where he alludes to the body as a "Tabernacle." 9. Jn. 2:19, 21. 10. Matt. 6:25 = Lk. 13:23. 11. Matt. 6:25 = Lk. 12:22. 12. Matt. 5:29b, 30b; cf. Mk. 9:43b, 47b. 13. Matt. 6:22, 23a = Lk. 11:34. 14. Mk. 10:8 = Matt. 19:6a. 15. Matt. 11:19 = Lk. 7:34. 16. Matt. 19:12. 17. I Cor. 11:24; Mk. 14:22 = Matt. 26:26; Lk. 22:19. 18. Rom. 8:2. 19. Prov. 4:23. 20. The best discussion of the meaning of these terms, not only in the Old and New Testaments, but in Greek literature in general, is by E. D. Burton, *Spirit, Soul and Flesh,* Chicago, 1918. 21. Matt. 6:25 = Lk. 12:22f. 22. Mk. 8:36f. = Matt. 16:26 = Lk. 9:25. 23. Lk. 17:33; cf. Matt. 10:39; and Matt. 16:25 = Mk. 8:35 = Lk. 9:24. 24. Matt. 10:28 = Lk. 12:4. 25. Mk. 12:30 = Matt. 22:37 = Lk. 10:27. 26. Mk. 10:45 = Matt. 20:28. 27. Mk. 14:38 =

Matt. 26:41. 28. Matt. 5:3. Other instances where *pneuma* designates psychical life proper are Matt. 26:4; Mk. 2:8; 8:12; 14:38; Lk. 1:47, 80. 29. E. D. Burton, *op. cit.*, p. 179. 30. Matt. 15:19 = Mk. 7:21. 31. Mk. 2:8. Cf. Matt. 9:4, "Wherefore think ye evil in your hearts?" Cf. Lk. 5:22. 32. Mk. 4:15 = Matt. 13:19 = Lk. 8:12. 33. Mk. 11:23. 34. This corresponds to our modern use of the word heart. The Greek word *splagchna (splagchnizō)* means about what we mean by heart and is so translated by E. J. Goodspeed, *The New Testament, An American Translation,* in Matt. 14:14; 18:27; Mk. 6:34; Lk. 1:78 (citing only the instances in the synoptic gospels). 35. Matt. 5:28. 36. Mk. 12:30 = Matt. 22:37 = Lk. 10:27. 37. Matt. 6:21 = Lk. 12:34. 38. Matt. 18:35. 39. Mk. 7:18b, 19a. 40. Mk. 7:21-23 = Matt. 15:18f. 41. Lk. 21:14. 42. Matt. 18:35. 43. Lk. 6:45 = Matt. 12:34f. 44. Mk. 7:6 = Matt. 15:8; quoting Isa. 29:13. 45. Matt. 11:29. 46. Lk. 8:15. 47. Matt. 5:8. 48. Mk. 10:2-12 = Matt. 19:3-9. 49. Ps. 95:8. 50. Mk. 8:17f. 51. Ezk. 11:19f. 52. Lk. 6:45 = Matt. 12:34f. 53. John Skinner, "The Cosmopolitan Aspect of the Hebrew Wisdom," JQR, xvii (1905), pp. 248f. 54. See Isa. 63:16; 64:6; Jer. 31:9; Mal. 2:10. See further, *infra* p. 186. 55. Deut. 11:26-28. 56. Deut. 30:15-20. 57. Prov. 11:27. 58. Sir. 15:14f. "Yetser is here used in a neutral sense (almost equivalent to free-will) in which lay the power of doing right or wrong." Box and Oesterley in Charles, APOT, *in loc.* Goodspeed renders: "Left him in the hands of his own decision." *The Apocrypha, An American Translation,* in loc. 59. Ps. Sol. 9:7, 9. 60. T. Jud. 20:1f. 61. Ab. 3:19. 62. Matt. 7:24-27 = Lk. 6:47-49. 63. Matt. 25:1-13. 64. Matt. 25:14-30; cf. Lk. 19:11-27. 65. Rudolf Bultmann, *Jesus,* N. Y., 1934, *passim*. 66. Cf. Jn. 2:25. 67. Matt. 15:10. 68. Lk. 12:57. 69. Lk. 21:30. 70. Matt. 7:16. 71. Matt. 7:19. 72. Matt. 5:45. 73. Matt. 16:2. 74. Matt. 5:13, 15. 75. Mk. 2:22 = Matt. 9:17 = Lk. 5:37f. 76. Mk. 2:21 = Matt. 9:16 = Lk. 5:39. 77. Matt. 6:19. 78. Matt. 6:27. 79. Matt. 5:36. 80. Matt. 12:12. 81. Lk. 15:18. 82. Jn. 8:11. 83. Matt. 5:45; cf. Lk. 6:35. 84. Matt. 12:11f; cf. Lk. 14:5. 85. Mk. 2:27. 86. Matt. 10:31 = Lk. 12:7. 87. Lk. 12:24 = Matt. 6:26. 88. Matt. 5:22. 89. Matt. 11:19. Cf. Lk. 7:34. 90. Mk. 8:2 = Matt. 15:32. 91. Mk. 6:34; cf. Matt. 9:36. 92. Lk. 10:30-37. 93. Lk. 19:2-10. 94. Lk. 18:2-6. 95. Mk. 12:40. 96. Lk. 16:19-31. 97. Matt. 25:43-45. 98. Mk. 12:31 = Matt. 22:39 = Lk. 20:27. 99. Job 1:9f. 100. Job 14:1. 101. Job 15:14. 102. Job 25:4. 103. Prov. 12:4. 104. Prov. 30:10-31. 105. Eccl. 7:26, 28. 106. G. A. Barton, *Ecclesiastes,* ICC, N. Y., 1908, p. 147. 107. Sir. 25:13, 15-20, 24-26; 26:6f.; 36:21-24; 22:3; 42:9, 11-14. 108. Sir. 36:21. 109. Sir. 36:24. 110. Sir. 26:13. 111. Sir. 25:24. 112. Gen. 3. 113. Gen. 6:2-4. 114. *Vid. infra,* Chap. 5, p. 111. 115. T. Reub. 5:6f. 116. T. Reub. 5:1. Cf. in full 3:10-6:4, and T. Jud. 15:5f. 117. C. G. Montefiore, *The Synoptic Gospels,* i. pp.

225-236, in re Mk. 10:2-12. 118. *Ibid.*, ii, p. 65, in re Matt. 5:32. 119. *Ibid.* 120. *Ibid.*, i, p. 388. 121. Lk. 10:39, *ēkouen,* imperfect of repeated action. 122. Aboth 1:4. 123. In Charles, APOT, ii, p. 691. Cf. Acts 22:3, in re Paul, brought up "at the feet of Gamaliel." 124. Mk. 10:15. 125. Montefiore, *op. cit.*, i, p. 237. 126. E. S. Ames, *Religion,* N. Y., 1929, p. 47. 127. II Tim. 1:10. 128. Matt. 10:28 = Lk. 12:4; Matt. 10:39 = Lk. 17:33; Mk. 8:35, 36, 37 = Matt. 16:25, 26 = Lk. 9:24; and Lk. 21:19. 129. Matt. 10:28 = Lk. 12:4. 130. Lk. 17:33, RVmarg. 131. Mk. 12:18-27 = Matt. 22:23-33 = Lk. 20:27-38. The place of the resurrection in the eschatological teaching of Jesus will be considered in Chap. 6. 132. Cf. I En. 1-36. 133. Deut. 25:5-10. 134. I En. 104:4; cf. Mk. 12:25 = Matt. 22:30 = Lk. 20:36. 135. I En. 104:6. 136. Lk. 20:38 = Mk. 12:27 = Matt. 22:32. A. E. J. Rawlinson, *The Gospel According to St. Mark,* London, 1925, p. 169: "It is possible that this was a stock argument of the Pharisees since it occurs in IV Macc. 7:19; 16:25." The date of IV Macc. is uncertain. It may be as early as 63 B.C., or as late as 70 A.D. I Abrahams, JE, viii, 244, thinks these passages in IV Macc. may possibly be due to Christian interpretation. 137. This is the very reasoning which the earliest Christian preaching used for the resurrection of Jesus himself, "whom God raised up, having loosed the pangs of death: because it was not possible that he should be holden of it." Acts 2:24. 138. Rawlinson, *op. cit.*, p. 169.

CHAPTER IV

1. Gen. 12:1-3. Cf. also 17:2, 4-6; 18:18; 22:17f.; 27:29; 28:14; 32:12. 3. Gen. 12:3. 4. See esp. S. J. Case, *Jesus—A New Biography,* pp. 142-145, 240. 5. Gen. 12:3. 6. Ps. 77:8. 7. Isa. 53:10. 8. Jer. 29:11. 9. J. R. Murray, "Promise," DCG, ii, 428f. 10. Cf. J. Denney, "Promise," DB, iv, 104. 11. Lk. 12:32. 12. Matt. 11:12. 13. Mk. 4:1-9 = Matt. 13:1-9 = Lk. 8:4-8. 14. Mk. 4:16 = Matt. 13:20 = Lk. 8:13. 15. Mk. 10:15 = Lk. 18:17. 16. Matt. 13:17 = Lk. 10:24. 17. Matt. 11:4f. = Lk. 7:22; cf. Isa. 61:1. 18. Mk. 13:32 = Matt. 24:36. 19. Mk. 13:20 = Matt. 24:22. 20. C. G. Montefiore, *The Synoptic Gospels,* 1927,[2] i, 26. 21. *Some Elements of the Religious Teaching of Jesus,* pp. 97f. 22. E. F. Scott, *The Gospel and its Tributaries,* Edinburgh, 1928, p. 57. 23. Gen. 16:7-13; 18:2; and many others. 24. Dan. 7:10; I En. 40:11; 60:1; 71:13. 25. II Bar. 59:11. 26: I En. 40. 27. II En. 22. 28. II En. 29:1, 3; II Bar. 21:6. 29. II Bar. 51:9. 30. I En. 60:17-19; Jub. 2:1. 31. II En. 14; 19; 5; 6; I En. 60:13f., 16-22. 32. Matt. 18:10. 33. Matt. 26:53; cf. 13:41; Mk. 8:38 (= Matt. 16:27 = Lk. 9:26). 34. Lk. 16:22. 35. Matt. 6:10. 36. Lk. 15:10. 37. Ps. 33:6. Cf. Sir. 42:15; Wisd. 9:1. 38. Isa. 9:7; 55:11. Ps. 147:15, 18; 148:8.

39. Ps. 107:20. Cf. Wisd. Sol. 16:12. Cf. K. Kohler, in JE, viii, 464. 40. Sir. 24:3-12. Quoted from E. J. Goodspeed, *The Apocrypha, An American Translation,* Chicago, 1938. 41. *Supra,* pp. 17f. 42. Cf. Gerald Friedlander, *Hellenism and Christianity,* London, 1912, p. 70. 43. Wisd. Sol. 10, 11. 44. Cf. Thos. Walker, *The Teaching of Jesus and the Jewish Teaching of His Age,* N. Y., 1923, pp. 46f. 45. Cf. Thos. Walker, *op. cit.,* p. 75. 46. Matt. 5:3-11; cf. Lk. 6:20-22. 47. Cf. e. g., Prov. 8:32, 34; 22:9; numerously in Psalms; Sir. 14:1, 2,20; II En. 42:10-14. Cf. additional instances of the beatitude form in Matt. 11:6 = Lk. 7:23; Matt. 13:16 = Lk. 10:23; Matt. 24:46 = Lk. 12:43; Matt. 16:17; Lk. 11:27; 13:37f.; 14:14f. 48. Cf. J. R. Murray, *loc. cit.* 49. Matt. 6:4, 6, 18. 50. Lk. 17:33; cf. Matt. 10:39. 51. Lk. 6:35. 52. Matt. 3:7-10 = Lk. 3:7b-9; Matt. 3:12 = Lk. 3:17. 53. Cf. Prov. 1:8, 10, 15; 2:1; 3:1, 11, 21; 4:10, 20; etc. 54. Mk. 10:24. 55. Matt. 5:45; cf. Lk. 6:35. 56. Matt. 6:25-34; cf. Lk. 12:22-31. 57. Matt. 6:32. 58. Matt. 6:33, 34a. 59. Rudolf Bultmann, *Jesus,* Berlin, 1926, p. 148. He cites specifically Lk. 12:22-31 (cf. Matt. 6:25-32); Matt. 10:29-31 (cf. Lk. 12:6-7); Matt. 5:45. 60. Mk. 9:23; Matt. 21:21 = Mk. 11:23 = Lk. 17:6. 61. Geo. T. Ladd, "Is the Universe Friendly?" Hibbert Journal, x (1911-12), p. 328. 62. For fuller discussion, *vid. infra,* Chap. 5. 63. Matt. 7:11 = Lk. 11:13. 64. Ex. 33:19. 65. Ex. 34:6-7a. 66. Matt. 5:45. This same truth found expression in the Stoic ethics, e.g., in Seneca: "If you would imitate the gods, give benefits even to the ungrateful; for the sun rises even upon criminals, and the seas are open to pirates." *De. ben.,* iv, 26, 1. 67. Mk. 4:28. 68. Mk. 4:26-29. 69. Matt. 7:7-11 = Lk. 11:9-11, 13. 70. Lk. 11:4. 71. *Supra,* p. 9. 72. Lk. 11:3 = Matt. 6:11. 73. Matt. 20:1-5. 74. Vs. 14. 75. Mk. 4:1-9 = Matt. 13:1-9 = Lk. 8:4-8. 76. Matt. 6:25-34 = Lk. 12:22-31. 77. Matt. 6:26 = Lk. 12:24. 78. Matt. 6:32 = Lk. 12:30. 79. Matt. 6:33 = Lk. 12:31. 80. G. T. Ladd, *loc. cit.,* p. 342. 81. Matt. 12:39f. 82. Lk. 11:29f. 83. Lk. 15:11-32. 84. Lk. 15:20. 85. Lk. 15:32. 86. Lk. 15:1f.

CHAPTER V

1. Gen. 1:31. 2. Matt. 7:30. 3. Cf. H. J. Wicks, *The Doctrine of God in Jewish Apocryphal and Apocalyptic Literature,* London, 1915, pp. 27-129. 4. Mk. 4:26-29. 5. Mk. 4:1-9 = Matt. 13:1-9 = Lk. 8:4-8. 6. Cf. B. W. Bacon, *The Story of Jesus,* N. Y., 1927, p. 212. 7. Cf. Sir. 29:27-31; 40:1-10. 8. Matt. 7:26f. 9. Lk. 13:4. 10. Matt. 4:6 = Lk. 4:10f. 11. So Prov. 3:11; 5:17; Sir. 32:14; Ps. 118. 12. Sir. 2:1-6; 4:15ff. 13. Sir. 11:28; Job 5:41; 20:10; 21:19; 27:14. 14. Sir. 11:26ff. 15. Cf. Job 31. 16. Eccl. 1:4; 3:14; 7:13. 17. Eccl. 2:24f.; 3:12, 22; 5:17-19; 7:14; 8:15; 9:7-10. 18. Cf. Eccl. 7:2, 15ff. 19. Cf. Ps. 73 on the prosperity of the wicked. 20.

Eccl. 3:21. 21. Mk. 10:17-31 = Matt. 19:16-30 = Lk. 18:18-30. 22. Mk. 10:22. 23. Mk. 10:23, 25. 24. The principal passages are Matt. 6:19-34 (cf. Lk. 11:34-36; 12:22-31, 33f.; 16:13); Matt. 19:16-30 = Mk. 10:17-31 = Lk. 18:18-30; Lk. 16:1-31; Lk. 10:38-42; Lk. 12:13-21; Lk. 19:1-10. 25. See the very admirable discussion of "The Hope of the Poor," by C. C. McCown, *The Genesis of the Social Gospel*, pp. 245-291, which reveals the social situation to which this phase of Jesus' teaching was directed. 26. Lk. 4:18. 27. Matt. 11:5 = Lk. 7:22. 28. Lk. 6:20. 29. A term adopted from D. C. Macintosh, *The Reasonableness of Christianity;* cf. fuller discussion *infra*, Chap. 9, pp. 191f. 30. Matt. 5:17f. 31. Gen. 3. 32. II Bar. 54:15. 33. IV Ezr. 3:21. 34. IV Ezr. 4:30. 35. Matt. 7:11 = Lk. 11:13. 36. Mk. 9:19 = Matt. 17:17 = Lk. 9:41; Matt. 12:39 = Lk. 11:29; Matt. 16:4. 37. Mk. 7:21ff. = Matt. 15:19. 38. Matt. 3:8 = Lk. 3:8. 39. Lk. 17:10. 40. Sir. 15:14. 41. *Yale Biblical and Semitic Studies*, N. Y., 1901, art. "Yetser Hara," pp. 93-156. Cf. also R. T. Herford, *Judaism in the New Testament Period*, London, 1929, pp. 92-95. 42. On the *yetser*, cf. IV. Ezr. 3:20-22, 26; 4:4, 30f.; 7:116-118. 43. Sir. 15:15. 44. See further Sir. 17:7-14 as setting forth the same theory of human choice; and cf. *supra*, pp. 63ff. 45. Sir. 21:11. 46. Sir. 4:28; 15:15; 21:11; T. Lev. 19:1; T. Jud. 20. 47. Mk. 7:20-22 = Matt. 15:18f. 48. *Vid.* C. W. Votaw, "Sermon on the Mount," DB, v, 25-28, on "Inner Righteousness." 49. Matt. 7:24-27. 50. A clear summary of the literature setting forth this doctrine is in Thos. Walker, *op. cit.*, pp. 194f. 51. I En. 18:1. 52. Matt. 12:43-45 = Lk. 11:24-26. E. D. Burton, *Spirit, Soul and Flesh*, p. 182, cites Matt. 12:43, 45; Mk. 5:8; 9:25 as instances where spirit is used in the sense of *demon*. 53. Matt. 8:29. 54. The instances of exorcism in the ministry of Jesus are as follows: (1) The Gadarene Demoniac, Mk. 5:1-20 = Matt. 8:28-34 = Lk. 8:26-39; (2) The Epileptic Boy, Mk. 9:14-29 = Matt. 17:14-20 = Lk. 9:37-43; (3) The Daughter of the Syrophoenician Woman, Mk. 7:24-30 = Matt. 15:21-28; (4) The Demoniac in the Capernaum Synagogue, Mk. 1:21-28 = Lk. 4:31-37; (5) The Man who was Dumb, Matt. 9:32-34; 12:22-24; cf. Lk. 11:14-16; (6) The Infirm Woman, Lk. 13:10-17. 55. Matt. 12:27 = Lk. 11:19 cite Jesus' reference to other exorcists. Cf. extended note on exorcism in S. J. Case, *Jesus—A New Biography*, pp. 358f. 56. Josephus describes the root "Baaras" and its use in exorcism, *War*, vii, 6, 3. Josephus details the methods of an exorcist named Eleazar and attributes his success to incantations taught by Solomon, *Ant.* viii, 2, 5. In *Ant.* vi, 8, 2, Josephus interprets King Saul's malady as demon possession. 57. Matt. 12:43-45 = Lk. 11:24-26, quoted *supra*. 58. Matt. 12:28. 59. Deut. 6:4. 60. Mk. 3:23-30 = Matt. 12:25-32 = Lk. 11:17-23. 61. Mark's statement, "He hath an unclean spirit," (3:30) misses the point of the charge against Jesus. That would be merely to say that Jesus was sick. His enemies did not charge Jesus merely with being weak instead of powerful. 62. So Matt.; Lk. "finger." 63. Matt. 12:28 = Lk. 11:20. 64. Matt. 12:27 = Lk. 11:19. 65. Matt. 13:24-30. 66. Matt. 5:39. 67. Lk. 15:11-32. 68. Lk. 15:1. 69. C. G. Montefiore, *The Synoptic Gospels*, ii, 520. 70. *Ibid.*, i, 43. 71. *Ibid.*, i, 39. 72. Heb. 12:2. 73. Montefiore, *op. cit.*, i, 16. 74. Isa. 51:9. Cf. also Job 26:12f. 75. C. F. Kent, *The Sermons, Epistles and Apocalypses of Israel's Prophets*, N. Y., 1910, p. 366. 76. Cf. L. W. King, *The Seven Tablets of Creation*, London, 1902, i, 71-73, on tablet iv, lines 103, 104. 77. G. A. Barton, *The Religions of the World*, Chicago, 1919,[2] p. 83. 78. Gen. 6:5, 7. 79. APOT, II, 171. 80. I En. 39:1, 2a; *54:7-55:2; 60; 65-69:25. Other Enoch passages on the deluge as the first world judgment are 10:4, 5, 12b; 91:5, 6f.; 93:4. See also Jub. 23:14. 81. S. H. Hooke (ed), *Myth and Ritual*, London, 1933, p. 195. 82. Lk. 17:26 = Matt. 24:37. 83. Cf. Mk. 13:5-20 = Matt. 24:4-22 = Lk. 21:8-24 on the climax of evil. 84. D. C. Macintosh, *op. cit.*, p. 51. 85. Mk. 12:1-9 = Matt. 21:33-41 = Lk. 20:9-16. 86. D. C. Macintosh, *op. cit.*, p. 158. 87. *Vid. supra*, p. 114.

CHAPTER VI

1. Among the principal passages setting forth the ethical ideal of the Old Testament prophets are: Amos 5:24; Hos. 6:6; Mic. 6:8; Isa. 1:10-18, 21-27; 11:1-9; Jer. 7:5-9; 9:23f.; Joel 2:13; Mal. 2:10, 15f.; 3:5; 4:2. 2. See F. C. Grant, *The Gospel of the Kingdom*, N. Y., 1940, p. 147. 3. *Vid. supra*, Chap. 1. 4. Mk. 6:15; 8:28; Matt. 16:14; 21:11; Lk. 7:16, 39; 9:8, 19; 13:33; 24:19. 5. Sir. 36:1-17. 6. Sir. 48:10. 7. Sir. 50:23f. 8. Sir. 36:11. 9. Sir. 35:18f. 10. Messiah is to be descended from Levi, not Judah: T. Reub. 6:7-12; T. Lev. 8:14; 18; T. Jud. 24:1-3; T. Dan. 5:10f.; T. Jos. 19:5-9. 11. T. Jud. 24:1; 25:3; T. Lev. 8:14f.; 18:10-12; T. Reub. 6:11f.; T. Dan. 5:10-12. 12. Wisd. Sol. 3:7f. 13. Wisd. Sol. 3:1-4; 4:2, 7-11; 5:2, 3a, 4, 5, 15. 15. Wisd. Sol. 3:16, 18. 16. *Vid.* R. H. Charles, *Eschatology*, pp. 165-170, 224-234, 306-312. 17. II En. 9; 42:7; 43:2f.; 49:1; 50:3; 51:1, 3; 52:2, 7f.; 63:4; 66:6. 18. Cf. Bern. Duhm, *Theologie der Propheten*, Bonn, 1875, p. 21; and R. H. Charles, *Eschatology*, pp. 108, 184-187. 19. Jer. 3-6. 20. Zeph. 1:7. 21. Ezk. 38:17. 22. Dan. 2:31f., 37f.; 4:7-12; 7; 8. 23. I En. 85, 86. 24. II Bar. 53, 56-69. 25. Sib. 3:819ff.; 2:5-290. 26. R. H. Charles, *Eschatology*, p. 183. Italics mine. 27. Cf. e. g., Dan. 3:17ff.; Jub. 21:22; T. Lev. 13:3, 708; II En. 63:2f.; T. Gad. 7:1; T. Jos. 18:2; T. Benj. 5:4, for assertions of this high ethical emphasis of apocalyptic in times of particular crisis. 28. The apocalyptical literature begins with Daniel, 165 B.C. 29. A. Deissmann, *The Religion of Jesus and the Faith of Paul*, N. Y., 1923, p. 75. 30. A. N. Wilder,

NOTES AND REFERENCES

Eschatology and Ethics in the Teaching of Jesus, N. Y., 1939, p. 4. 31.
Rev. 1:3; 22:19. 32. T. Lev. 14:4. 33. R. H. Charles, *Eschatology,* p. 194.
34. S. Angus, *The Mystery Religions and Christianity,* p. 64. 35. *The
Gospel and its Tributaries,* Edinburgh, 1928, p. 46. 36. Heinrich Weinel,
Biblische Theologie des neuen Testaments, Tübingen, 1928,[4] p. 58. 37. Jer.
16:1-9. 38. Matt. 6:3-5 = Lk. 6:41f.; cf. Matt. 23. 39. Matt. 5:44 = Lk.
6:27, 35. 40. Cf. Rudolf Bultmann, *Jesus,* Berlin, 1926, p. 199. 41. Jub.
23:13f., 16, 18f., 22-24, 26. 42. II Bar. 70:3, 5, 8, 10. 43. IV Ezr. 5:1-12;
6:21f., 25-28. 44. Mk. 13:7-20 = Matt. 24:6-22 = Lk. 21:9-24. 45. Cf.
esp. Lk. 17:31, 33. 46. C. F. Kent, *Sermons, Epistles and Apocalypses of
Israel's Prophets,* N. Y., 1910, pp. 42f. Cf. esp. chap. vii, "The Historical
Development of Israel's Messianic Ideals," pp. 39-48; also "Messianic and
Eschatological Prophecies," pp. 467-503. 47. The most important passages bearing on the subject of the messiah are: Isa. 11:1-10; 9:2, 6, 7;
chaps. 51-53; Dan. 7; Mic. 5:2-4; Ezk. 34:11-31; Jer. 23:5f.; Zech. 9:9f.
The order in which these are listed is not chronological, but rather the
order of importance; nor is the list intended to include all Old Testament messianic passages. 48. Sib. 3:655f.; T. Reub. 6:11; T. Dan.; Ps. Sol.
17:23, 28, 32, 34f., 38; Zad. Frag. 2:10; 8:2; II Bar. 39:7; 72:2; 70:9. I En.
49:4; 46:3; 47:3; 51:3; 62:2, 3, 5; 69:27-29. 49. T. Naph. 4:5; T. Jud.
24:1; Ps. Sol. 17:35; T. Jud. 24:6; Ps. Sol. 17:31, 41; T. Jud. 24:1; I En.
36:2; 53:6; 39:6; 62:2; 49:2; 48:4; 46:3; 71:14; 105:2. 50. Ps. Sol. 17:42;
18:8; T. Lev. 18:7; T. Jud. 24:1. 51. I En. 49:1, 3. 52. Sib. III, 652-654.
53. I En. 90:37f. 54. I En. 48:10; 52:4. 55. I En. 37:2; 53:6; cf. Acts.
3:14; 7:52; 22:14. 56. I En. 40:5; 45:3f.; etc. Cf. Lk. 9:35; 23:35. 57. The
principal Enoch passages are: I En. 46:2-6; 48:2-10; 62:5-14; 63:11;
69:26-29; 71:14-17. 58. Cf. Charles, APOT, ii, p. 214. He adds: "As (1)
Judge he has righteousness (38:2; 39:6; 53:6; 46:3; cf. Ps. 45:4-7; 72;
Isa. 11:3-5), wisdom (49:1, 3; 51:3) and power (49:3; 62:6). As (2)
Revealer he will bring to light the invisible worlds of righteousness and
sin (46:3; 49:2, 4) and raise the dead (51:1; 61:5) and judge all (51:2;
55:4; 61:8; 62:2f.; 69:27). As (3) Champion he upholds, vindicates, and
rewards the righteous (39:7; 48:4, 7; 51:5; 53:6; 62:7, 8, 14, 15)." 59.
II Bar. 30:1. 60. IV Ezr. 7:28. 61. IV Ezr. 13:2-13. 62. II Bar. 36-40,
53-70; IV Ezr. 10:60-12:35. 63. IV Ezr. 13:10; cf. Ps. Sol. 17:27. 64. Mk.
13:26f. Cf. Matt. 24:30f. and Lk. 21:27f. 65. Lk. 17:22, 24, 26. Matt. has
transferred this material and incorporated it in the eschatological discourse; cf. Matt. 24:27, 37, 39. 66. Prof. C. W. Votaw, in an academic
lecture on "The Teaching of Jesus Concerning Himself," Feb. 6, 1929,
at the University of Chicago. 67. Jub. 4:26; cf. 1:29; 23:26-28. For full
discussion of the Son of Man passages in the synoptic gospels, with bibliog-
raphy, cf. S. J. Case, *Jesus—A New Biography,* pp. 363-371. This author

considers that if Jesus used the expression "Son of Man," "either it was in an impersonal sense, meaning mankind in general, humanity, or else he appropriated a technical term already in vogue." But Case questions whether Jesus used the term even in the third person. Thos. Walker, *op. cit.*, pp. 148-181, holds that Jesus used the term of himself in some instances in the sense in which it is used in Ezekiel as a term for "the prophet." "He seems to have accepted the idea of himself as 'the prophet' under the name of the 'son of man.' " Cf. further, Montefiore, *Synoptic Gospels,* i, 64-80, excursus on "Son of Man." 68. E. F. Scott, *The Kingdom and the Messiah,* p. 20. 69. Isa. 65:17f. 70. Isa. 66:22. 71. Jub. 4:26; cf. 1:29; 23:26-28. Charles dates 104-101 B.C. 72. I En. 91:16f. Charles dates 104-101 B.C. 73. I En. 45:4f. Charles dates 94-64 B.C. 74. II Bar. 32:6. 75. II Bar. 51:3. 76. II Bar. 48:50. 77. II Bar. 44:12. 78. II Bar. 51:8. 79. II Bar. 57:2. 80. IV Ezr. 7:75. 81. II Pet. 3:13. 82. Rev. 21:1. Cf. Charles, *Eschatology,* pp. 127-9, 249, 260, 333. 83. Matt. 5:5. 84. Matt. 6:10. 85. Lk. 17:26 = Matt. 24:37. 86. Isa. 26:19. 87. Dan. 12:2. 88. Charles, *Eschatology,* p. 131, accepts Cheyne's dating, 334 B.C., but states that even if Duhm, Marti, and Kennett are right in assigning it to the close of the second century, B.C., the doctrine itself is most probably not later than the third century, B.C. 89. Esp. vs. 2. 90. Before 170 B.C. So Charles, *Eschatology,* p. 213. 91. I En. 25: 4-6. 92. I En. 25:6. 93. I En. 10:20-22. 94. I En. 10:21. 95. I En. 22:10; 27:2. 96. Dated 166-161 B.C. by Charles, *op. cit.,* p. 220. 97. Dated 109-106 B.C. by Charles, *op. cit.,* p. 224. 98. T. Benj. 10:6-9. 99. Dated 104-95 B.C. by Charles, *op. cit.,* p. 250. 100. I En. 91:10; cf. 92:3. 101. I En. 103:3f. 102. I En. 104:2. 103. I En. 104:4. 104. I En. 104:6. 105. Dated 94-64 B.C. by Charles, *op. cit.,* p. 260. 106. I En. 51:4. 107. I En. 62:15f. 108. I En. 51. 109. I En. 62:14-16. 110. Dated 7-29 A.D. by Charles, *Eschatology,* p. 301. Cf. 301-303. 111. Jub. 23:31. 112. II En. 22:8-10. Dated 1-50 A.D. by Charles, *op. cit.,* p. 315. 113. *War,* II, 8, 14. 114. II Bar. 30:2-5. 115. II Bar. 49:2. 116. II Bar. 50:2. 117. IV Ezr. 7:32. 118. Mk. 12:18-27 = Matt. 22:23-33 = Lk. 20:27-38. 119. Amos 3:2, 11f.; 5:1-3, 5, 18, 27; 6:7; 7:11; 9:4. The Day of Yahweh is conceived both as a day of punishment and as a day of blessing. It is called *"that day,"* Isa. 17:7; 30:23; 28:5; 29:18; Hos. 2:18; Mic. 2:4; 4:6; 5:10; Zech. 9:16; 14:4, 6, 9; "that time," Jer. 31:1; 33:15; 50:4; Zeph. 3:19f.; Joel 3:1; *"the day,"* Ezk. 7:10; Mic. 3:6; "the time," Ezk. 7:12. 120. Against Israel: 2:6-21; 8:1-4; 9:8-20; 17:1-11; 28:1-4. Against Judah: 1:10-17, 21-26; 3:1-15; 5:8-24; 28:14-22; 29:1-4; 30:8-17; 31:4. 121. Zeph. 1:2f., 8-18; 2:1-6; 3:8. 122. Zeph. 3:12f. 123. Cf. esp. Jer. 1:11-16; 37:6-10; 25:15-24; 23:7f.; 24:5f.; 3:13, 19-25. 124. Ezk. 38, 39. 125. Joel 3:1, 2, 12. 126. Cf. esp. I En. 10:1-13; 16:1; 19:1; 22:4, 11; 25:4. 127. Cf. esp. I En. 90:20-27. 128. Cf. esp. I En. 41:1; 44:6; 63; 38:5; 48:9f.; 62:12; 53:3-5; 54:1f., 6; 55:4; 38:3; 41:2; 45:2, 6. 129. Jub.

23:11. 130. Cf. esp. I En. 91:12-17; 94:9; 98:10; 100:4; 103:8; 104:5.
131. Esp. vss. 27-39. 132. II En. 7:1; 18:6; 39:2; 40:12; 48:8; 50:4; 51:3;
52:15; 58:5; 60:4; 65:6; 66:7. 133. IV Ezr. 7:31-44; 12:34. 134. Matt. 3:7,
10, 12 = Lk. 3:7, 9, 12. 135. Matt. 3:8, 10 = Lk. 3:8f. 136. Lk. 3:10-14.
137. Mk. 13:32 = Matt. 24:36. 138. Mk. 13:30 = Matt. 24:34 = Lk.
21:32. 139. Lk. 21:34; Matt. 24:50 = Lk. 12:46. 140. Matt. 6:4, 6, 18.
141. Matt. 25:31-46. 142. Matt. 25:37-39. 143. See further Matt. 16:27;
Mk. 9:41 = Matt. 10:42. 144. Matt. 25:14-30; cf. Lk. 19:12-26. 145. Matt.
10:28 = Lk. 12:5. 146. Matt. 12:41 = Lk. 11:32. 147. Matt. 12:42 = Lk.
11:31. 148. Matt. 18:35. 149. Lk. 13:27 = Matt. 7:23; Matt. 25:41-45.
150. Matt. 11:21-24 = Lk. 10:12-15. 151. Matt. 25:41, 46. 152. Cf. Bousset,
Jesus, p. 121. 153. Cf. e. g., the camel and the needle's eye, Mk. 10:25 =
Matt. 19:24 = Lk. 18:25. 154. Matt. 5:48.

CHAPTER VII

1. Isa. 1:24-26. 2. Zeph. 3:13f. 3. Jer. 23:4-6; 3:15; 12:14f.; 4:2; 16:19;
12:16f. 4. Cf. esp. the Servant Songs, Isa. 42:1-4; 49:1-6; 50:4-9; 52:13-
53:12. 5. Cf. esp. Ps. 22:27-31; 65:2, 5; 86:9; 87:4f., 7. 6. Mal. 3:12, 17.
7. Isa. 19:21, 23-25; variously dated; 275 B.C., Cheyne; others later.
8. Ezk. 11:17-21; 36:25-32; 17:22-24; 21:27; 34:23-31; 37:21-28; 38; 39.
9. Isa. 14:1-3; 66:12-16, 18-20; 60:10, 12, 14; 61:5; 4:2-6; 27:6; 29:16-
24; 35:1-10; 59:15-20; 63:1-6. 10. Hag. 1:8; 2:6-9, 20-23. 11. Zech.
1:18-21; 3:8f.; 6:12; 2:12f.; 8:23; 7:9f.; 8:16f.; 2:11; 8:20f., 23. 12. Joel
3:17f., 20. 13. Dan. 7:21f.; 12:1-3; 7:9, 11f., 14, 22, 27; 2:44. 14. I En.
25:4-6; 10:7, 16, 20-22; 25:5; 10:21. 15. I En. 11. 16. Cf. esp. II Macc.
7:14, 29. Dated 100-40 B.C. by Charles, *Eschatology*, p. 273. 17. I En.
90:28-36. Dated 166-161 by Charles, *op. cit.*, p. 220. 18. I En. 91:12-17.
19. I En. 91:10, 16f.; 92:3. 20. Esp. Ps. Sol. 11:1-8; 17:50. 21. Ps. Sol.
3:16. 22. Jub. 23:11, 27-29. 23. Assump. Mos. 10:3-10. Dated 7-29 A.D.
by Charles, *Eschatology*, p. 301. 24. II En. 32:2-33:2; II Bar. 29:4-30:1;
39:3-40:3; 73:1-4; 74:1f. 25. IV Ezr. 7:28. 26. I En. 58. Dated 94-
64 B.C. 27. Cf. C. H. Dodd, *The Parables of the Kingdom*, N. Y., 1936,
pp. 34f. 28. E. F. Scott, *The Kingdom and the Messiah*, p. 92. 29. Cf.
Kirsopp Lake, *Landmarks of Early Christianity*, London, 1920, pp. 24f.
See also F. C. Grant, *The Gospel of the Kingdom*, N. Y., 1940, pp. 147,
149. 30. Cf. esp. Matt. 5:22, 28, 32, 37, 44; 6:3, 6, 18. 31. Lk. 11:41.
32. Cp. the rendering of Goodspeed: "The kingom of God is not coming visibly, and people will not say, 'Look! Here it is!' or 'There it is!'
for the kingdom of God is within you;" and Moffatt, "The Reign of
God is not coming as you hope to catch sight of it; no one will say,
'Here it is,' or 'There it is,' for the Reign of God is now in your midst."
Lk. 17:20f. 33. Matt. 13:33 = Lk. 13:20f. 34. Cf. S. J. Case, *Jesus—*

A New Biography, p. 436. 35. Matt. 13:44. 36. Matt. 13:45. 37. Mk.
10:14 = Matt. 19:14 = Lk. 18:18. 38. Matt. 5:3; cf. Lk. 6:20. 39. Mk.
12:34. 40. Matt. 21:31. 41. Matt. 8:5-11 = Lk. 7:1-9. 42. A. Boyd Scott,
Christ: The Wisdom of Man, London, 1928, pp. 122f. 43. Mk. 1:15 =
Matt. 4:17. 44. Matt. 11:4f. = Lk. 7:22. 45. Matt. 12:28 = Lk. 11:20.
46. Matt. 6:33 = Lk. 12:31. 47. Lk. 10:18. 48. Matt. 13:17 = Lk. 10:24.
49. The Baptist is meant. "A difference like that all-important iota of the
Council of Nicea. To John the kingdom is imminent, to Jesus it is immanent." B. W. Bacon, "New and Old in Jesus' Relation to John," JBL,
xlviii (1929), p. 70. 50. B. W. Bacon, *The Story of Jesus,* N. Y., 1927,
p. 215. 51. Matt. 24:36 = Mk. 13:32. 52. Mk. 9:1 = Matt. 16:28 = Lk.
9:27. 53. Matt. 6:10 = Lk. 11:2. 54. Matt. 8:11; cf. Lk. 13:29. 55. Mk.
14:25 = Matt. 26:29 = Lk. 22:18. On the futurity of the kingdom see
also Matt. 13:43 and 20:21. 56. Mk. 9:47. 57. Matt. 18:9. 58. Mk. 9:43;
cf. Matt. 18:8. 59. Matt. 7:14. 60. Cf. further Mk. 10:15 = Matt. 18:3 =
Lk. 18:17. 61. Mk. 10:17 = Lk. 18:18; cf. Matt. 19:16, "that I may have
eternal life." Goodspeed renders *klēronomēsō* in Mk. 10:17 and Lk. 18:18,
"make sure of." Moffatt retains "inherit." 62. Lk. 18:24 = Mk. 10:23;
cf. Matt. 19:23. 63. Mk. 10:30 = Lk. 22:30; cf. Matt. 19:29, "shall
inherit eternal life." Goodspeed renders *klēronomēsei* in Matt. 19:29,
"share." Moffatt retains "inherit." 64. Matt. 25:34. Goodspeed here
renders *klēronomēsate* "take possession of." Moffatt: "come into your
inheritance." 65. C. G. Montefiore, *The Synoptic Gospels,* i, xcvii.

CHAPTER VIII

1. *Supra,* pp. 118f. 2. Matt. 25:34. 3. *Vid. supra,* p. 119. 4. Lk. 17:26 =
Matt. 24:37. 5. Lk. 17:28. 6. Gen. 18:20f.; 19:1-28. 7. Lk. 21:11 = Mk.
13:8 = Matt. 24:7. 8. Isa. 54:9. 9. Gen. 7:1. 10. Am. 5:15; cf. also
Am. 5:3. 11. Isa. 7:3. 12. Isa. 4:2ff.; 6:13; 17:4-6; 28:5; 37:31f. 13. Isa.
17:6; cf. J. A. Bewer, *The Literature of the Old Testament,* N. Y., 1922,
p. 117, note. 14. Zeph. 3:11-13. 15. Ezk. 17:22f. 16. Eccl. 1:9. 17. Lk.
17:26 = Matt. 24:37. 18. Lk. 18:8. 19. Mk. 9:10 = Matt. 17:17 =
Lk. 9:41; Matt. 12:39 = Lk. 11:29; Matt. 16:4. 20. Lk. 16:1-12. 21. Lk.
18:1-8. 22. Matt. 5:25f. = Lk. 12:58f. 23. Mk. 10:42 = Matt. 20:25 =
Lk. 22:25. 24. Matt. 11:12 = Lk. 16:16. 25. Lk. 18:7. 26. Lk. 16:9.
27. Lk. 16:15. 28. Matt. 5:3-12 = Lk. 6:20-26. 29. Mk. 6:34 = Matt.
14:14 = Lk. 9:11. 30. T. W. Manson, *The Teaching of Jesus,* Cambridge,
1931, p. 234. 31. Lk. 12:32. 32. Mk. 4:26-29. 33. Mk. 13:32 = Matt.
24:36. 34. Matt. 13:33 = Lk. 13:20f. 35. Lk. 10:17. 36. Lk. 10:20. 37. Cf.
D. C. Macintosh, *Social Religion,* N. Y., 1939, p. 83. 38. Lk. 10:3 = Matt.
10:16. 39. Matt. 9:37 = Lk. 10:2. 40. Mk. 6:6-11 = Matt. 9:35-10:16 =
Lk. 9:1-5; 10:1-12. 41. Matt. 7:14 = Lk. 13:24. 42. Matt. 22:14. 43. Matt.

22:1-14 = Lk. 14:15-24. 44. Matt. 11:25 = Lk. 10:21. 45. *Vid. supra,* pp. 156f. 46. Tobit 4:15. 47. Aristeas §207. 48. Babylonian Shabbath, 31a. 49. Reported in Eusebius, *Praeparatio Evangelica,* viii, 7:6. 50. Prov. 24:29. 51. Prov. 20:22. 52. Isa. 3:10f.; 53. Lev. 24:19. 54. Obad. 15. 55. Matt. 26:52. 56. Matt. 5:38-41 = Lk. 6:29. 57. Matt. 7:8 = Lk. 11:10. 58. Matt. 7:2. 59. Lk. 6:38. 60. The citations of the Golden Rule from all such literature may be found in R. E. Hume, *The World's Living Religions,* N. Y., 1924, pp. 265-267. 61. *Sacred Books of the East,* 39:91. 62. According to Diogenes Laertius, "Lives and Opinions of Eminent Philosophers," 5:21; Bohn Library translation, 188. 63. See F. C. Grant, *The Gospel of the Kingdom,* N. Y., 1940, p. 170. 64. Rom. 11:5. 65. I Cor. 3:9. 66. H. E. Fosdick, *A Guide to Understanding the Bible,* N. Y., 1939, p. 149.

CHAPTER IX

1. Notably G. F. Moore, *Judaism;* Strack-Billerbeck, *Kommentar zum Neuen Testament aus Talmud und Midrash,* München, 1922; J. Klausner, *Jesus of Nazareth,* N. Y., 1925; C. G. Montefiore, *The Synoptic Gospels,* 1927², who stresses the originality of Jesus as well as his dependence. 2. *Op. cit.,* p. 384. 3. Notable articles are: Frank C. Porter, "The Problem of Things New and Old in the Beginnings of Christianity," JBL, xlviii (1929), pp. 1-23; E. F. Scott, "The Originality of Jesus' Ethical Teaching," *ibid.,* pp. 109-115; C. G. Montefiore, "The Originality of Jesus," Hibbert Journal, xxviii, 1 (Oct. 1929), pp. 98-111. 4. F. C. Porter, *loc. cit.,* p. 2. 5. Wm. E. Hocking, *Human Nature and its Remaking,* New Haven, 1918, p. 275. 6. "Far the greater number of parallels are superficial, affecting the forms of thought more than the thought itself. . . . These resemblances can be so piled up as to make a convincing case for dependence, but they prove little more than that Jesus lived in Palestine in the first century." E. F. Scott, JBL, xlviii (1929), p. 110. In similar vein F. C. Porter, *ibid.,* p. 5: "One who is looking for parallels to the greater sayings of the gospels will meet many surprises and disappointments. Most of the material here collected (i. e., in Strack-Billerbeck) consists of illustrations of rabbinical usage of words and phrases, indispensable to the interpreter, yet leaving the question of newness very much as it was. For the newness of a great teacher, prophet, or poet, whose words have been creative through the ages and are still living and powerful, is to be discerned only by one who feels the distinction and greatness of the personality behind them." 7. Paul Wernle, *Jesus,* Tübingen, 1917, p. 99. 8. "The Originality of Jesus," Hibbert Journal, xxviii, 1 (Oct. 1929), p. 100. 9. "The Originality of Jesus," Hibbert Journal, xxviii, 1 (Oct. 1929), p. 101. 10. *Vid. infra,* pp. 186f. 11. *Some Elements in the*

Religious Teaching of Jesus, p. 107. *Vid. supra*, p. 117. 12. Mk. 7:15. Cf. *Synoptic Gospels*, i, 131. 13. Mk. 10:35-45. Cf. *Synoptic Gospels*, i, 253. 14. Mk. 10:2-12 = Matt. 19:3-9; cf. Lk. 16:18. Cf. *Synoptic Gospels*, ii, 65. 15. Matt. 20:1-16. Cf. *Synoptic Gospels*, ii, 275. 16. *Ibid.*, ii, 325. 17. Quoted *infra*, p. 186. 18. "The Originality of Jesus," Hibbert Journal, xxviii, 1 (Oct. 1929), p. 109. 19. *Ibid.* 20. Maurice Goguel, *op. cit.*, pp. 557f. 21. *Vid. supra*, pp. 173-179. 22. *Vid. supra*, p. 58. 23. *Vid. supra*, pp. 74, 183. 24. Vol. II, pp. 201-211. 25. C. G. Montefiore, "The Originality of Jesus," Hibbert Journal, xxviii (Oct. 1929), p. 104. A kindred view is expressed by G. A. Barton, *Studies in New Testament Christianity*, Philadelphia, 1928, pp. 44, 46. 26. Lk. 15:11-32. *Vid. supra*, p. 97. 27. C. G. Montefiore, *Some Elements in the Religious Teaching of Jesus*, 57f. 28. John Baillie, *The Interpretation of Religion*, N. Y., 1929, p. 444. 29. Matt. 5:48. 30. *Vid. supra*, p. 8. 31. *Vid. supra*, p. 155. 32. *Vid. supra*, pp. 51, 100f. 33. *Vid. supra*, pp. 66-68, 73, 110. 34. *Vid. supra*, pp. 110, 115. 35. *Vid. supra*, pp. 91-98. 36. *Vid. supra*, pp. 156f. 37. *Op. cit.*, p. 43. The other three are pessimism, non-moral optimism, and mere meliorism; these are rejected because unreasonable. 38. *Op. cit.*, p. 46. 39. Matt. 6:33 = Lk. 12:31; Lk. 12:5 = Matt. 10:28. 40. John Baillie, *The Place of Jesus Christ in Modern Christianity*, p. 101. 41. *Vid. supra*, pp. 115ff. 42. *Vid. supra*, pp. 156ff. 43. *Vid. supra*, p. 150. 44. *Vid. supra*, pp. 132f. 45. S. J. Case, *Jesus—A New Biography*, pp. 438f. 46. Jer. 31:33f. 47. Ezk. 36:26f. 48. Joel 2:28. 49. Ps. 51:10. 50. Ps. Sol. 17:28-51. 51. Jub. 1:23-25. 52. Mk. 1:15 = Matt. 4:17. 53. Matt. 25:34.

CHAPTER X

1. Matt. 7:11 = Lk. 11:13. 2. Lk. 11:4; cf. *supra*, p. 93. 3. Col. 1:3. 4. Translation by A. R. Gordon in *The Old Testament, An American Translation*, ed. by J. M. P. Smith, Chicago, 1927; altering LORD = Yahweh. 5. Sir. 1:4, 9f. Quoted from E. J. Goodspeed, *The Apocrypha, An American Translation*, Chicago, 1938. 6. Sir. 24:3-12. Quoted from Goodspeed, *op. cit.* 7. Wisd. 7:22. Quoted from Goodspeed, *op. cit.* 8. Wisd. 7:24-8:1. Quoted from Goodspeed, *op. cit.* 9. *Vid. supra*, p. 21. 10. Matt. 11:25-27 = Lk. 10:21-22. 11. Lk. 11:49 = Matt. 23:32. 12. Matt. 23:37-39 = Lk. 13:34-35; quite in the mood of Jer. 7:25, II Chron. 36:15ff., and Prov. 1:23-33. 13. Lk. 7:35; cf. Matt. 11:19. In several writings, B. W. Bacon emphasized the Wisdom Christology of the Second Source; cf. esp. *Studies in Matthew*, N. Y., 1930, pp. 203ff. 14. John 1:1-18. 15. Col. 1:15-17. 16. I Cor. 1:24. 17. I Cor. 1:30. 18. Col. 2:3. 19. Heb. 1:1-3. 20. Col. 1:28. 21. II Cor. 10:5. 22. Col. 3:16; Moffatt translation. 23. Col. 4:5; Moffatt translation. 24. Acts of Paul, 2:6.

INDEX

INDEX

INDEX

Hades, 37, 41, 43
Haggadah, 12
Haggai, 152
Hagiographa, 8
hagioi, 178
Ham, 36
Healing, 112
Heart, 56, 57, 60, 61, 110
    hardened, 61
    of flesh, 62
Heaven, 153
Heavens, 38-42, 138
Hebrew language, 13
Hebrews, Epistle to, 206
Hellenism, 30
Herford, R. T., 12-13, 27, 73
Hillel, R., 174
Hinduism, 177
History, Philosophy of, 147, 163, 164

Idealism, 80, 93, 98
    Ethical, 194-195
Immanence, 86-87, 188
Immortality, 74-76, 145
Incarnation, 200-207
Insight, Moral, 66-67
Inwardness, 100-101, 155, 169, 188-189, 198
Isaac, 77
Isaiah, 146, 151, 152, 166
    Second, 117, 118, 151, 165
Israel, 134, 153

Jacob, 77, 86
Japheth, 36
Japhia, 28
Jehoshaphat, Valley of, 147
Jeremiah, 3, 125, 132, 146, 151, 195
Jerusalem, 11, 36, 86, 139
    New, 152
Jesus, Childhood of, 10
    education of, 12-19

Jesus—(*Continued*)
    originality of, 8, 180-184
    youth of, 10
    as teacher, 19-20, 22, 28, 29, 63
    as thinker, 7, 32-33
Jesus' use of Scripture, 13-15
Jewish war, 78
Job, 3, 5, 34, 46, 47, 51, 102-103
Joel, 147, 152, 196
John the Baptist, 24, 27, 105, 108, 148, 157, 169
Jonah, 96
Jubilees, 129, 134, 139, 144, 147
Judea, 31
Judgment, 141, 146-150, 192

Kant, 1
kardia, 59
Kent, C. F., 134
Kingdom of God, 43, 80, 82, 83, 150, 151-162, 171-172, 188, 191, 193
Klausner, J., 180
Koheleth, 5, 71, 103, 104; see also Ecclesiastes
Kuchavim, 40

Law, 115, 169
Lazarus, 43, 85
Legalism, 128-129
Levi, 69
    Testament of, 39
Leviathan, 37
Life, Eternal, 173
Logia, 22
Logos, 204-205
Lord's Prayer, 93
Luke, 11, 23
Lyceum, The, 23

Maccabees, Second, 152
    Fourth, 4
Macintosh, D. C., 51-52, 121, 191

[235]